THE LAND AND PEOPLE OF

Indonesia

The Republic of Indonesia is one of the most remarkable
countries in the world. It lies halfway around the globe from
America, and is a vast cluster of more than 13,000 islands,
some of which are among the world's largest; its breadth is
greater than the distance from New York to San Francisco,
and it has the fifth largest population in the world. This is
the once-fabled land of the Indies, the Spice Islands of
romance that lured European adventurers around the world.
Its magical charm continues to draw visitors from all countries. But Indonesia is of great practical importance also, as
a major source of natural resources for the world, and as the
largest member of the Association of Southeast Asian Nations (ASEAN).

Along with a survey of Indonesia's rich cultural background
and early history, this new revised edition—with an updated
map and new photographs—describes the nation's present
government and economy, and the outlook for its future.

Portraits of the Nations Series

Other books in this series deal with:

Portraits of the Nations Series

THE LAND AND PEOPLE OF

Indonesia

NEW REVISED EDITION

Datus C. Smith, Jr.

J. B. LIPPINCOTT

NEW YORK

*For valuable assistance in preparation of this revised edition,
the author is deeply grateful to his daughter, Karen Houston Smith;
to Professor Hewitt Panaleoni of SUNY/Oneonta; and most especially
to Ismid Hadad of "Prisma," Jakarta.*

Library of Congress Cataloging in Publication Data
Smith, Datus Clifford, date
    The land and people of Indonesia.

(Portraits of the nations series)
    Summary: Introduces the history, geography, people,
culture, government, and economy of the country covering
more than 13,000 islands and having the fifth largest
population in the world.
    1. Indonesia—Juvenile literature.   [1. Indonesia]
I. Title.
DS615.S5 1983   959.8   82-48964
ISBN 0-397-32048-5
ISBN 0-397-32049-3 (lib. bdg.)

Contents

TAIWAN

INDONESIA

MANILA

REPUBLIC
OF THE
PHILIPPINES

PACIFIC OCEAN

HALMAHERA   IRIAN JAYA   Jayapura

Ternate
TIDORE

M A L
U

CERAM
AMBON   EWAB

SULAWESI
(CELEBES)   ARU

Banda Sea   K
U

TANIMBAR

jung Pandang   WETAR   BABAR
FLORES   ALOR
Dili
TIMOR

MBA   ROTI

AUSTRALIA

Don Pitcher

I

Islands in the Sea

Indonesia's population is the fifth largest in the world. Only China, India, the Soviet Union, and the United States have more people than Indonesia's estimated 154 million. And the length of the country from one end to the other is greater than from New York to San Francisco, while the distance from north to south is about like that from Minneapolis to New Orleans.

In spite of that great size, Americans have tended to think of Indonesia as a small country because they have known so little about it and because it has been so new in current world affairs.

This book tries to introduce Americans to that attractive green land that is halfway around the globe from us, directly on the Equator and between the continents of Asia and Australia.

Indonesia is the largest "archipelago country" in the world. It is not a solid landmass but a vast cluster of more than 13,500 islands, of which more than 6,000 are inhabited. Many of the islands are small (the total figure includes some no larger than a tennis court), but mighty Kalimantan, which we used to call Borneo, is the third largest island in the world. And Sumatra is about a thousand miles from tip to tip.

This beautiful country of islands is washed by the waters of the Pacific and Indian oceans and the South China Sea. The countries that are the closest neighbors are Singapore and Malaysia to the

north, the Philippines to the northeast, and Australia to the southeast.

This is the fabled land of "the Indies," the Spice Islands of
history and romance. Famous names that appear in the story include
Marco Polo, Kublai Khan, Ferdinand Magellan, Sir Francis Drake,
Saint Francis Xavier, and a legion of daring adventurers from Portugal, Spain, Holland, and Britain in the Age of Discovery. This was
the source of the great wealth of the Netherlands and the site of the
once enormous empire controlled by that tiny country. In the nineteenth century Yankee traders came to the area and took marvelous
treasures home. Nowadays Indonesia is of interest to the entire
world.

About 90 percent of the population is Muslim. We will talk
later about the Indonesian people and the fascinating surroundings
in which they live. But let us first take a quick survey trip around
the islands for a bird's-eye view of the whole country.

Geographers divide up the islands of the Indonesian archipelago in different ways. Politically the country is divided into
twenty-seven provinces, like our states. For us it is perhaps easiest
to think of them in four groups:

1. *The Western Islands* of Sumatra, Kalimantan, and Java.
2. *The Lesser Sunda Islands,* a chain running from Java toward
   Australia.
3. *The Eastern Islands,* including Sulawesi and the many islands in the Maluku group that stretches over about a thousand miles of ocean between the Philippines and Australia.
4. *Irian Jaya,* the western part of the island of New Guinea.

Starting in the upper left-hand corner of the map (page viii–ix),
we first encounter the thousand-mile-long island of Sumatra. It has
mountains along its west side, close to the shore. The eastern side
slopes down to flat savannah and marshes, though with many big
areas that people have learned to put to use. In the southern part

of the island there have been important developments in growing irrigated rice, much as in Java; and great plantations of rubber, sugar, and other commercial crops are also found on Sumatra.

The island is one of the major sources of oil and natural gas in Indonesia, and smaller islands off its southern coast, especially Bangka and Billiton, produce large amounts of tin.

There are about 30 million people in Sumatra, and they are of very different sorts. At the northern end of the island are the ruggedly independent people of Aceh. Somewhat south of them are the Batak, who have a completely different culture, and many of whom are Christians.

About halfway down the west side of the island are the Minang-kabau people, whom we will meet again later. On the east side are descendants of the original Malay people; their language and culture are quite like that of the Malaysians living across the strait from them. In this area, near the city of Pekanbaru, is one of the major oil fields and a refinery operated as an American concession. There is a mixture of tribes and languages at the southern end of Sumatra. Of Sumatra's five large cities, Medan has a population of almost 1.5 million, Palembang 800,000, Padang 500,000, and Tanjungkarang 300,000.

Kalimantan (the Indonesian part of the island we used to call Borneo) does not have many great mountains, but much of it is hilly and forested. Borneo as a whole is the third largest of all islands in the world (following Greenland and New Guinea), but not all of it belongs to Indonesia. Along the northern edge are the two Malaysian territories, Sabah and Sarawak, and the small independent territory of Brunei. Oil and rubber are produced in both parts of Kalimantan. In the west there is an area of farmland worked by descendants of Chinese who came in originally as gold miners.

There are not many more than 7 million people in Kalimantan's huge area. Through much of the northern and central parts the

One of more than a hundred volcanoes in Indonesia

people are Dayaks, with a language of their own and living a quite primitive life of hunting, fishing, and "shifting agriculture"—that is, they will clear and plant ground, raise crops there for a few years, and then move on after the natural chemicals are exhausted. Of the few cities on the whole island, Banjarmasin is the largest, with a population of over 400,000, and Balikpapan is next, with 280,000. Kalimantan is a significant producer of timber and wood products, which are among Indonesia's major exports.

Java is by all odds the most populous of all the islands: 95 million, including Madura, the small island at the eastern end, which for government purposes is treated as part of the Province of East Java. Java is one of the lushest and most densely populated places on earth. A great volcanic chain of mountains runs the length of the island. In certain sections some of the area is lost to wasteland, but elsewhere there is a marvelous development of rice terraces and plantations of sugar, tea, coffee, rubber, and other crops.

The people who are called Javanese and use Javanese language are at the extreme western tip and in the eastern two-thirds of the

One of Jakarta's modern hotels

island. The western third of the island is occupied by the Sundanese people, with their own distinctive language and culture. The Madurese have their own language, though it is closely related to Javanese.

Four of Indonesia's five largest cities are on Java. Jakarta (formerly called Batavia by the Dutch) is the national capital. It has a population of over 6.5 million, making it one of the biggest cities in the world. Like New York City, Jakarta has attracted people from so many other parts of the country and from abroad that it has a true cosmopolitan spirit and a culture of its own.

Many Indonesians, as well as foreigners, criticize Jakarta and say they certainly would hate to live there, just as many Americans criticize New York. There is surely less natural courtesy and friendliness, less gracious adjustment to the problems of living, in those huge cities than in some of the country areas or smaller towns in both countries. In Jakarta, however, strong neighborhood associations and the tradition of mutual assistance help to keep alive some of the qualities of the areas from which the people came.

Another large city on Java is Surabaya, a growing center of

Auto traffic in downtown Jakarta

manufacture, with more than a million people, at the eastern end of Java. The city of Bandung, whose special reason for world fame we will mention later, has about 1.5 million people. On the north coast is Semarang, with about a million population. Yogyakarta is a small city, but it is important in our story, as it has been called "the cradle of Javanese culture," and it was the capital during the revolution against the Dutch.

Going eastward from Java, we come to the Lesser Sunda chain of islands, which the Indonesians call Nusa Tenggara. First is the beautiful island of Bali, which many people think is as close to paradise as they are likely to come before going to heaven. This is the one part of Indonesia still Hindu in religion. The distinctive culture and delightful scenery have made it one of the great tourist attractions in Asia. Balinese architecture, music, dance, costuming, carving, and textiles are famous all over the world.

Working eastward along the chain, we go from Bali to Lombok, Sumbawa, Sumba, Flores, Timor, and many smaller islands. The eastern half of Timor was Portuguese, the only surviving trace in the

East Indies of Portugal's imperialist effort of the fifteenth and sixteenth centuries. But in 1976 it was taken over by Indonesia and
integrated into the Republic as the twenty-seventh province. There
are no large cities in the Lesser Sundas, and the total population is
about 8.5 million.

In the islands in the northeast quarter of the country, the
biggest is Sulawesi, which we used to call Celebes. It is the most
curiously shaped large island in the world. Some people say it looks
like an orchid. Its far-flung arms go out in such odd directions that
early European traders thought it was a group of islands rather than
just one. The plants and animals of Sulawesi include varieties found
nowhere else in the world. The principal city, Ujung Pandang, once
famous for spice smuggling and piracy, is now a dynamic center of
trade and education, and is a central point of communication and
transport between east and west in Indonesia. (The former name
Makassar appears in our vocabulary in an odd way: the cloth cover

Traditional houses in a Christian village in Sulawesi

for head-rests on New England chairs was called an "antimacassar" because it protected the fabric from the oily heads of returned Yankee seafarers who used oil from Makassar on their hair.) The total population of Sulawesi is about 10.5 million.

In Maluku, formerly called the Moluccas, the Spice Islands of the past, the biggest island is Halmahera, with a shape almost as odd as Sulawesi's. Another large island is Ceram. The provincial capital is Ambon, a beautiful small island city overlooking a handsome harbor, with jungle-clad slopes rising behind the city.

Christian missions were set up in Maluku very early, and the Spanish/Portuguese Catholic influence was followed by Dutch Protestantism. In the Maluku islands that are heavily Christian there has been change in the form of folk art, and some of the traditional forms of music and the dance have been lost. Even long periods of Christian influence, however, have failed to wipe out many familiar customs and beliefs. The total population of Maluku is only 1.5 million.

The easternmost section of the archipelago, Irian Jaya, is the western half of the island of New Guinea. The eastern part of the island is Papua New Guinea, a newly independent nation in an area formerly held by Australia. Irian Jaya has rich linguistic and cultural variety.

In the agreement in 1949 about the other islands, Holland and Indonesia were not able to settle whether or not Irian Jaya also would become part of Indonesia, so it was left for later agreement. Holland continued to hold the area, but Indonesia pressed its claim in the United Nations and elsewhere. Holland refused to negotiate through the years but finally, in 1962, under pressure of world opinion and threatened by possible military action from Indonesia, agreed to a settlement. After a brief period under UN administration, Irian Jaya became part of Indonesia in 1963. A former American ambassador, Ellsworth Bunker, played an important part on the UN's behalf in the negotiations leading to this result.

2

The Green Land
and Its People

The physical setting of Indonesian life is dramatic. Many of the great mountains are volcanoes; this is known as the most volcanic region of the world. In dense green jungles on the mountainsides, or on the plains or in the swamps below, are such wildlife as monkeys, tigers, thirty-foot-long pythons, wild boars, crocodiles, strange birds of handsome plumage, and an endless variety of small animals and insects of the most delicate beauty.

Some of the land is so fruitful that an entire family can live on the produce of a plot smaller than an American farmer would think worth planting. The whole year is a growing season in this tropical region, so a piece of land may produce three crops a year.

Exotic plant life is everywhere. Rice is the chief food for the majority of the people, and the rice paddy on plains or terraces is typical of the scene in Java and much of Sumatra. Coconut trees grow by the million, and one constantly sees bamboo, papaya, and banana.

For much of the time until recent years, Indonesia was the biggest producer of natural rubber in the world. Most of it has grown on huge rubber plantations owned by companies. Other plantations grow sugarcane, palm oil, tobacco, coffee, tea, and cinchona (the

A rice field in Java

source of the medicine quinine). Pepper comes from Indonesia, and so do other spices that we shall later see played a big role in the country's history. Tapioca, rattan, teakwood, and kapok (for upholstery) are other products. Timber is the number-one non-mineral export. Delicious fruit is available in every season, and in varieties whose very names are unknown to us.

Beneath the soil is still more wealth. Oil is the most important mineral product and, together with natural gas, is a major factor in Indonesia's income from abroad. But there are also tin, nickel, coal, and bauxite (the source of aluminum), and lesser amounts of salt, manganese, gold, silver, and other metals. Iron, uranium, and copper resources are believed to exist in considerable quantity, but they have not yet been adequately developed. Gas, which can be exported in liquid form (called LNG), produced in Arun, Aceh, and the Natuna islands, has recently developed into one of Indonesia's most valuable exports, second only to oil. Tin is the most valuable metal resource, but its export has declined somewhat. Indonesia's estimated tin reserve of 825 million metric tons is one of the largest in the world. Uranium ore is believed to be present in Kalimantan and the Nusa Tenggara islands.

Along the coastline, which is one of the longest in the world, and in the waters offshore, Indonesia draws on the riches of the ocean. Besides the growing fish industry on the seacoast, there is an inland fish culture by which fish are handled as a "crop" in ponds or in the waters of a rice paddy between crops of grain.

Green is the color of the landscape, except for a narrow strip of barren rocky land in some of the southern islands of Nusa Tenggara and southern Maluku. There are always accents of brilliant flowers and flowering trees and, in some sections, the red-tile roofs of houses.

The islands in the west, Sumatra, Java, and Kalimantan, are set in shallow seas, often only 200 feet deep, and much of the land along their shores is swamp and marsh. This suggests what the geologists say is a fact: that these major western islands were part of the Asian mainland not too many thousand years ago. In fact, this part of Indonesia might be considered still part of the mainland, even though portions of it are buried under a few hundred feet of water.

The islands to the east of this continental shelf, however, are the tops of incredibly steep mountains going right up from the floor of very deep seas. In some cases there is a difference in altitude of 30,000 feet between an ocean deep and an island mountaintop not a hundred miles away. This region is geologically "young," and mountain-building is still going on. Earthquakes are frequent, and there are two or three mild tremors every day, as well as occasional severe ones.

Volcanoes are found in a great crescent-shaped line going the length of Sumatra and Java and then sweeping northward into the Philippines. There are more than a hundred active volcanoes in the country, about half of them in Java, and countless dead cones from former times. At the bottom of Sumatra is a tiny island which is all that is left of one of the world's most famous volcanoes. This is Krakatoa, which blew up in 1883, destroying much of the island and causing tidal waves and dust clouds that circled the globe. A new eruption produced a little island of volcanic ash in 1928, and it is called Anak Krakatoa ("child of Krakatoa").

The volcanoes are so dramatic that they interest us for their own sake, but they also give the key to all life in Indonesia. There are two kinds of lava that come from volcanoes. The sort called "acid" makes wasteland that is very poor for growing things. But the sort called "basic" gives a rich soil on which crops thrive.

The wonderful productivity of Java, and of parts of other islands, results from the deep layers of volcanic soil, plus the steady rainfall and warmth. The areas that are the richest in agriculture tend to become the richest culturally and the strongest politically. So we might say that the enormous power of volcanoes when they are active is not lost, but continues to affect the life of the people for centuries after they themselves are cold and quiet.

The main features of the Indonesian landscape, aside from the changes made in it by man, are the mountains, the tropical "rain forests" that are the same the year round, a few "monsoon forests" with some seasonal change, the "swamp forests" along the flat shorelines and sometimes continuing far inland, and the areas of brushy grassland or "savannah." This last is a flat land with few trees and little vegetation except shrubs and giant grasses. Such areas are of little natural use to people, and the same is true of the jungle swamps.

Plant life is of amazing variety. Wild orchids grow as parasites on trees in the jungle and on backyard racks in the cities. There are giant ferns as tall as trees. The banyan, a species of fig, seeds itself in a crotch of another tree, putting down roots to the ground; eventually the other tree is destroyed, leaving the fig high in the air, supported by aerial roots that come down from its branches, making eerie caverns of the space they enclose. Fantastic vines called lianas have been known to grow to the thickness of a man's thigh and to lengths of hundreds of feet.

The largest flower in the world, *Amorphophallus titanum*, is a native of Sumatra. The bloom is as tall as a man and sometimes a yard in width. In the same area grows *Rafflesia*, also enormous, named for an English governor we will meet later.

Plenty of rain and steady warmth keep things green in much of the country. Some sections have no dry season at all. Bogor, a small city near Jakarta, has an average of more than 300 thunderstorms each year. Some places have a rainfall of 160 inches per year. (For comparison, San Francisco normally has about 22 inches, Chicago 33.)

Too continuous a rainfall can be harmful, because the thick

One of Sumatra's giant flowers. This one is as tall as a man.

jungle swamps of mangrove trees that result are no help to man. Also, even aside from the swamps, vegetation grows so fast that unless there is ceaseless effort, land cleared for farming quickly goes back to its jungle state. But in quite a bit of Indonesia the amount of rain is exactly right for crops. In such places, as on the island of Java, there is almost unbelievable fertility of a useful sort.

Because of the nearness of the sea, the actual thermometer reading is lower than we might expect in the tropics. In almost a hundred years of record-keeping in Jakarta, the highest temperature in history was 96 degrees, and the average is about 80. Even so, the steaming heat in low-lying areas seems to the foreign visitor to be almost impossible to bear when he first meets it. Morning and evening humidity are almost always in the 90s. At higher altitudes, however, the temperature and humidity are lower and the air more bracing.

Indonesia's position on the Equator makes the temperature in any one place about the same all the year round. In many sections not more than three degrees separate the average of the warmest from the coolest month. Seasonal change is much less than that resulting from height above sea level. The thermometer may drop about one degree for each 300 feet above the sea.

Also, because of nearness to the Equator there is a difference of less than an hour between the longest and shortest days of the year, as compared with nearly six hours' difference in the latitude of New York.

The land is rich, especially in some of the islands, yet because of the enormous population there are areas of great poverty. This is especially so in the largest cities, where people have lost the support of subsistence agriculture that they had when living on the land. For countries like Indonesia, money figures of personal income, though significant for economists, are not very useful in telling us the quality of life of individual citizens. It is hard to estimate the usable income of people in countries such as Indonesia where homegrown food may be more important for many families than income in the form of money. Even with allowance for that, however, Indonesians were formerly considered by economists to be among the poorest people on earth. With improvement in recent years, however, the average Indonesian's annual income has risen to a figure which the World Bank estimates at $370 and some private international banks even higher, at $415.

Some people think that, because of the growing population, the situation will become worse. Others are hopeful that, if some kind of balance can be found between growth of population and increase of food supply, life can become better. These people put their faith in reclaiming wasteland; in improving the yield of crops, especially rice, and in further advance in the growing of fish; in building up industries, aided by electricity from waterpower; in a movement to the islands that are less thickly settled; and—most important of all—in a slowing down of the rate of increase of population. Family planning is progressing.

The center of Indonesian national life is on the remarkable island of Java, with which the small island of Madura is usually associated. Approximately 95 million people live on Java-Madura—which is in area about the size of Alabama and comprises about 7 percent of Indonesia's land area. It is one of the most intensely cultivated spots on earth. Ingenious systems of irrigation have helped nature's own generosity so much that the land supports more than 1,795 people to the square mile—which compares with about 62 to the square mile for the United States, 202 for Indonesia as a whole, and about 560 for India, which is tragically overpopulated.

Because Java is so thickly populated, there has been an effort to get the Javanese to emigrate to other islands, especially Sumatra and Kalimantan, where there is much empty space. It is thought that some of the present wasteland could be adapted to support people, just as parts of the Great American Desert in our Southwest were converted to such use. The movement out from Java has not yet

Family procession to a Hindu cremation ceremony in Bali

been very great, however, and has by no means kept up with the population growth on Java itself. Although 1,795 people to the square mile live on Java, in Sumatra the density is only 150 and in Kalimantan about 33.

As in all countries, the population in Indonesia is more interesting than anything else. The ethnic and geographical variety of Indonesia is reflected in the people. But the majority are brown-skinned, with rich black hair and dark eyes. They are intelligent, good-humored, warm people who love to be in groups and traditionally have great skill in interpersonal relations. They are persistent in their hard-won sense of national identity.

The majority of the people are of a stock called Indonesian or Malay, but with some mixture of blood of Indian origin, as well as bits of Chinese, Arab, and European.

More than nine-tenths of the people are Muslim in religion, that is, followers of Mohammed, the Arab prophet of Islam. His teachings in the Holy Koran came to these remote islands through trading vessels in past centuries. But the influence of Hindu, Buddhist, and even earlier beliefs is still strong. And Western influence, through the Portuguese, British, Dutch, and more recently other Europeans and Americans, can be seen in religion, education, business, and science. At least in the cities it is also evident in such details of daily life as movies, blue jeans, lipstick, and Coca-Cola.

The way of life of the Indonesians is highly varied. The capital city of Jakarta has a cosmopolitan intellectual and business community, combining knowledge of their own literature, arts, and philosophy with ability in international trade, friendships in Western countries, and understanding of many brands of modern technology. In contrast, in Irian Jaya, the former West Irian, are tribes just a few steps from the Stone Age, living by the most primitive agriculture and by hunting and fishing.

Typical old-and-new scene: motorcycle on a traditional rustic bridge

It is with good reason that the country has as its national motto the words *Bhinneka Tunggal Ika,* meaning "Unity in Diversity," which is just about like our own *E Pluribus Unum,* "One Out of Many."

Love of independence is of course the strongest force holding the parts of the country together. Another is the sense of the importance of religion, regardless of whether Islam, Christianity, or Hinduism. But something needing special mention is the national language.

There are more than two hundred languages spoken in family and village life. But a single national language came to general use as part of the independence movement. We shall discuss the language further in a later chapter, but this may be a good place to mention two things about pronunciation. Most letters are pronounced about as you might expect, but there are two rules worth learning:

c is pronounced CH as in "chip"
sy is pronounced SH as in "shoe"

After independence, English replaced Dutch as Indonesia's official foreign language, and there is a rapidly growing knowledge of our language.

Indonesians have an absolute passion for education. Denial of the chance for most of them to learn during the rule of other countries made them especially eager for education after they started running their own affairs.

Before independence, only about 7 percent of the Indonesians could read and write, and a mere handful had a higher education. Few members of the older generation were well enough trained to qualify for senior leadership of this great country, and that made it hard to organize the life and work of the Republic. Old and young were determined that the new generation would be literate, educated, and, as required, technically trained.

Though few could read and write in the past, there was a real literary tradition in some of the languages, especially Javanese. And there have been other forms of cultural life throughout the centuries. Although these were actually more intricate than mere reading and writing, they required no formal training in school classrooms. These were the wonderful arts of music, dance, theater, sculpture, painting, architecture, batik-making, and other crafts that continued right through the whole period of foreign rule.

The Republic was established in 1945. It survived periods of great trouble, to the surprise of much of the world. Getting independence was in itself a glowing achievement. But the country had a hard time working out a stable and effective political system. Governing oneself is always a harder job than breaking loose from foreign control. But the most difficult task after independence was how to develop the country itself, how the government could help combat the problems of poverty, illiteracy, and unemployment faced by the majority of the population.

In our own early history, the end of the War of Independence was the beginning of a difficult period. Indonesia, likewise, has been troubled by indifference, bad management, inefficiency, dishonesty, and the selfish interests of special groups and regions. And Indonesia has had special problems we never knew about, because the pressure of world politics is far greater in this age.

But Indonesia has gone right on through crisis after crisis. There is reason for hoping that, no matter what may happen, these wonderful people will come out serenely on the other side of their difficulties. They have a shining goal in the ideals of their Republic. These are the Five Principles (called *Pancasila*) whose symbols are on the national coat of arms: Belief in God, Humanitarianism, Nationalism, Democracy, and Social Justice.

To learn the history of this green land, and the achievements and problems and hopes of its people, we should turn back to the beginning.

3

From the Beginning

The story of human life in Indonesia is one of the oldest in the world, and its beginning may be traced from thousands of years before history was written. Almost from the first there are signs of at least some of the characteristics that we see in Indonesia today.

Southeast Asia, the region in which Indonesia is the largest and most important country, has not usually played a big role in world affairs in its own right. But it has served through many centuries as a meeting place of races, cultures, religions, languages, and commerce. World War II and the period of the fighting in Vietnam and Kampuchea have been only some of the many times when military forces from outside the area have fought with each other in Southeast Asia.

Commerce is the key to much of the story. The modern American businessman going to Indonesia is in a tradition that has lasted for thousands of years. And contact through foreign trade explains much of the richness and variety in Indonesian culture.

How did it all start? No one can say exactly how life began on earth, or the exact steps of evolution that led to the earliest form of *Homo sapiens,* or where that happened first. It is no longer as certain as it once seemed that Asia was the birthplace of man, but it still appears likely that tropical Southeast Asia was at least one of the places where the great evolutionary process occurred.

One of the figures in the drama even bears an Indonesian name. The so-called "Java Man," whose fossil remains were found in 1891, is perhaps the most famous of the pre-human forms known as *Pithecanthropuss erectus.*

As our scientific knowledge has increased, and as the remains of other types have been found, in Java and elsewhere, much has been learned about these early creatures, and about the true human beings who followed them. Indonesia is a rich source for the earliest chapter of the human story.

Present-day Indonesians seem not to be descendants of those earliest human inhabitants of their country, but rather of a people who came from the outside many thousands of years later. A series of great migrations into Southeast Asia has been traced by study of fossils, stone implements, and other remains of ancient culture.

Of those waves, the one that left the largest number of living descendants today, and indeed supplied the basic stock of the present Indonesian people, was a race appropriately called Indonesians.

The oldest of these Indonesians are believed to have come from southwest China, and to have moved about 4,000 years ago into the land that is now the Indonesian archipelago. Scholars note that there were two types of those ancient Indonesians. The people in the second group are often called Coastal Malay, as they settled along the shore, while the earlier arrivals tended to keep to the highland interior.

For both types the terms "Indonesian" and "Malay" are often used interchangeably, and these people are of the racial type seen most often nowadays in Southeast Asia.

There was some connection of the ancient Indonesians with Mongol peoples in the homeland, and there is evidence of Chinese trade in the area of present-day Indonesia back to at least 100 B.C.

But India was more important than China in Indonesian history. The influence was stronger, and its effect was lasting. At the time of the first Chinese trade, or even earlier according to some experts, there was Indian trade and perhaps there were settlements of colonists from India. For some time Indian traders went to the islands in search of gold, silver, and tin, and eventually some of them decided to settle permanently.

For lack of formal history books to give the facts about this early contact, scholars turn to other sources. Evidence is given not only by the writing in Indian script on stone monuments in Sumatra and Java, but also by what appear to be references to the islands preserved in very old Indian literature.

By the seventh and eighth centuries A.D., kingdoms had grown up in Sumatra and Java with close connections with India. This remarkable Hindu-Indonesian civilization developed steadily, and then continued strong for nearly seven centuries, until the time of the general conversion to Muslim beliefs. In fact, the Hindu-Indonesian influence did not disappear with the coming of Islam, and it is still evident. It can be seen in many phases of Indonesian life right down to the present day. The name normally used for this culture is Hindu-Javanese, because Java was its center, but the Hindu influence spread to all the islands during that time.

Traders and settlers from India brought not only Hinduism but also Buddhism. And Chinese traders, though less numerous, also brought Buddhist influence. It was in central Java during the eighth and ninth centuries A.D., under the kings called the Shailendras, that there was an absolute flower-burst of artistic activity. Architecture was one of the arts in which the Javanese excelled, and it is for some of the great buildings that Buddhism in Java is best remembered today.

The greatest of all the monuments in Indonesia, the mighty temple of Borobudur in Java, dates from this period, and gives the modern beholder a vivid feeling of the force that this religion exerted in Javanese life.

But we should not think of central Java in the Borobudur period as having become entirely Buddhist. During all of Indonesian history

Aerial view of the Buddhist temple of Borobudur (modern trestles in background were used in restoration)

the lines dividing cultures and religions have been hazy. Old beliefs and old ways continued in the Indies, no matter what religion was officially accepted. Each new religion took on some color of the old. And the former faith, where it continued, became modified to include parts of the new ritual or belief Social patterns, also, influenced religion, and vice versa.

The political history of the islands is just as mixed. A kingdom would come to power in a local area, gain control of some neighboring territory, and then disappear or merge in a greater monarchy. A majority of the "kings" were no more than tribal chieftains, and their "nations" merely tribes able to exercise power over a nearby region for a little while. Some of the kingdoms, however, especially those in Java and along the Strait of Malacca, lasted for longer periods, had influence in mainland Asia as well as in the islands, and showed the pomp and ceremony of royal courts in a fairy tale.

One of the early kings deserving our notice even in this quick survey was King Airlangga of East Java, an eleventh-century monarch whose name is well known in Indonesia today, though he reigned shortly before the Norman Conquest of Britain. Legends about him are familiar to the common people, and Westerners call him an "Indonesian King Arthur." His name has been given to one of the leading universities of present-day Indonesia.

Another of the great names, in this case from the fourteenth century, is likewise used by a modern university. This is Gajah Mada, Prime Minister of the kingdom of Majapahit. He was one of the first statesmen in Indonesia in the modern meaning of the term. He had a vision of one country for all the islands, and did in fact succeed in bringing a large part of Indonesia under the rule of his king.

This Majapahit Empire, which was the biggest Indonesian nation until the birth of the Republic six and a half centuries later, showed in its origin a familiar pattern of interference in Indonesian affairs by foreign countries. Time after time through history, world events, even if far away, have had strong effect in the islands. An example of this can be found at that early time, even before the coming of the first Europeans.

The fabulous Kublai Khan of China is the chief actor in this drama. Kublai was ruling a large section of mainland Asia from his picturesque court in Peking (now called Beijing) when, late in the thirteenth century, he started a drive to the south. It was a movement that later centuries would have called "imperialist expansion." Smaller nations were conquered or scared into submission, and then were included in a system of satellites. One after another they fell under Kublai's control.

But a king in Java, Kertanagara, refused to give in, and even offered to help a threatened neighbor. This and other Javanese signs of independence were too much for Kublai. He ordered an attack on the island kingdom. More than two years went into getting ready for this amphibious operation, which was to be the greatest military venture in Indonesia up to that time. Hundreds of vessels and more than 20,000 troops were said to be involved.

When the attack finally came in 1293, it had a most unexpected result. King Kertanagara had died before the Chinese reached Java, so the invaders were not able to discipline the king as they had planned. They were, however, persuaded to help one of the parties fighting for the throne left vacant by Kertanagara's death. But then they were tricked into a position in which their large army, spread through the countryside, was ambushed by Javanese forces. Before long, the Chinese and their armada withdrew. The only result was that they had helped launch the powerful Majapahit Empire, which was eventually guided to greatness by Gajah Mada. Indonesia was not always so fortunate in disposing of invaders.

It was just a year or so before Kublai's attack on Java that the first European visited another of the islands. This was Marco Polo. He was returning with his father from the court of the Great Khan in China when he touched at northern Sumatra.

Marco's visit is interesting to us not only as the first European presence in Indonesia, but because he noted in passing something that we now see was of great importance to the future of the islands. Marco wrote that although Sumatrans in general were pagan worshipers of idols, "many of those who dwell in the seaport towns have been converted to the religion of Mohammed by the Saracen merchants who constantly frequent them."

Muslim traders from the Persian Gulf and the Red Sea as well as from India had been making voyages to the Indies for centuries before Marco's observation. As time went on, more and more came, some of them as settlers; this was especially true along the Strait of Malacca, the greatest trading channel of Southeast Asia.

Ports in Sumatra and Java were centers for exchanging goods between the East and the West. They dealt in the produce of China as well as of the islands. But the spices of Maluku, in the eastern part of present-day Indonesia, were what produced an excitement like a gold rush.

Enormous profits could be made from a single voyage. The taste of Europeans and Near Easterners demanded larger and larger amounts of pepper, cloves, and nutmeg, as well as rare herbs, scented woods, and the oils extracted from them. Some of these products of Maluku were found also in India or elsewhere, but for many of them at that time there was not a single other source known to Europeans.

The produce of these Spice Islands was carried from the Indonesian trading centers to India. Then it went by overland caravan to bazaars in the Near East, and then on to Europe, or sometimes directly to Arab and Persian ports without using the overland route through India.

It was natural that the first strongly Muslim area should be right where Marco Polo saw it, along the Strait of Malacca. As the map on pages viii–ix shows, it is a narrow waterway between the island of Sumatra and the Malay Peninsula, the nearest part of mainland Asia. Any seafarer heading for the Spice Islands, or intending to turn northward to China, would naturally go "down the slot" of the Malacca Strait, right past the island at the tip of the Malay Peninsula

Gathering cloves in Maluku

that is the site of present-day Singapore (though the city itself did not come into being until centuries later).

As local rulers and chiefs along the Strait adopted the teachings of Mohammed's holy book, the general population followed them. In accordance with Indonesian custom, however, there was no clean break with the past. Indeed, there were Muslim mosques in the architectural form of Hindu-Javanese temples, and Muslim tombs bearing Hindu symbols.

By the end of the fourteenth century, the powerful kingdom of Malacca, alongside the Strait, was firmly committed to the Muslim faith. During the fifteenth century there was a rapid spread to many of the islands. From that time onwards, the Indies have been overwhelmingly Muslim, in spite of the centuries of Christian contact and the influence of the Portuguese, Dutch, and British. The island of Bali, to which a Javanese Hindu prince fled when the Muslim religion triumphed in Java, became and remained an island of Hinduism surrounded by other religions. There are Christian sections in the country also. But the islands in general have been Muslim since the fifteenth century; and Indonesia has the largest Muslim population of any country in the world.

After the Indies had accepted Islam, and while Indians, Arabs, and Persians were busily engaged in the spice trade, western Europe was on the brink of the Age of Discovery. A shorter route to "the Indies" (that is, to Maluku, the source of the spices) was one of the chief reasons for the perilous voyages undertaken by the Spanish, Portuguese, and English. As we know, the purely accidental result was the discovery of America. Although the theory of reaching the East by sailing west was entirely sound, the first direct contact with Indonesia by European vessels came about in another way—by the eastward voyages of Portuguese ships around Africa.

The fifteenth-century Portuguese prince known as Henry the Navigator not only studied navigation and geography, but also sponsored voyages of exploration. Portuguese ships pushed down the west coast of Africa ever farther and, after Henry's death, went eastward around the Cape of Good Hope, then to the island of Madagascar, and finally, in 1498 under Vasco da Gama, across the Indian Ocean to India.

But the conquistador who really established Portugal's power in the Indian Ocean and beyond was the great admiral and governor, Alfonso de Albuquerque, whose name is as famous in Eastern history as Cortez's and Pizarro's in the West. Albuquerque set up the naval base at Goa, on the west coast of India, and from there undertook the conquest of Malacca on the west coast of the Malay Peninsula. It was he who directed Portugal's boisterous entry into the Indonesian story.

Separate pieces of world history were beginning to come together. Albuquerque's attack on the kingdom of Malacca was not only a commercial venture but a kind of continuation of the Crusades. The Christians in the West had been battling Moors and Turks, so it seemed natural and proper for the Portuguese to continue the struggle against these other Muslims half a world away.

Whatever the religious tone, however, the real goals were the spices and other riches of the Indies. Possession of the "tollgate" of Malacca gave control of the trade from the Spice Islands and the seaborne commerce of the Far East with India, the Middle East, and Europe.

At this time—about a hundred years before the Pilgrims reached Plymouth in the other half of the world—Portugal was the strongest power in the Indies.

4

Europe Comes to

the Indies

Capture of the Muslim stronghold of Malacca alongside the Strait established the Portuguese with the powers of a tollgate-keeper. It also put them conveniently near the pepper gardens of Sumatra. But the cloves and nutmegs of Maluku were still 2,500 miles away.

The Portuguese made mistakes from the very beginning. They hated Islam, and they had nothing but contempt for the Malays and Indonesians. Their first act after taking Malacca was utterly shocking to good Muslims: they built a fortress from Muslim gravestones. Then they staged a series of executions. Later their admiral undertook a campaign of general piracy in the Indian Ocean. From start to finish the adventurers left a record of brutality and betrayal. The British and Dutch in their turn made costly errors also, but Portuguese action was often without reason. Political disaster came eventually, and finally loss of most of the commerce itself.

Once they set up power in Malacca, the Portuguese undertook expeditions to Maluku for the spices. In Maluku the two kingdoms ruling most of the spice sources were Ternate and Tidore, the latter rather easygoing in religious matters, but the former bitterly anti-Christian. It is an oddity of history that, in spite of the crusading spirit of the Portuguese, it was with Christianity's enemy, the kingdom of Ternate, that they made a kind of alliance. And it was also there in Ternate that they established their first fortress in the Spice Islands.

Aside from Malacca and Maluku, the Portuguese put down few roots, and even in Maluku they got into serious trouble. Christian-Muslim enmity made things worse. The famous Catholic missionary, Saint Francis Xavier, visited the Spice Islands in the 1540s and missions were established. Many communities went over to Christianity. But as always in Indonesia, "conversion" could be a matter of power politics rather than belief. A local king with a sharp eye for business or military advantage might find it wise to adopt a new faith. His subjects would swing over with him, though not necessarily changing their customs or beliefs very much, and perhaps swing back a few years later.

For a time the island of Ambon in Maluku was both a military and a religious center for the Portuguese in the eastern islands. But at the very moment when rival Europeans were pushing into the area, Portuguese troubles with the local kingdoms reached a crisis. Anti-Portuguese revolts flared up, anti-Christian movements started, and the shaky structure of Portugal's eastern empire began to fall apart.

The final act opened with the treacherous murder in 1570 of a great Indonesian king, Sultan Hairun of Ternate, who had extended his power over a vast area from the Philippines southward. He was slain while under the supposed protection of a safe-conduct. The vengeance sworn against the Portuguese by his son, and the hatred felt by other kings, did much to hasten the end.

Although the Portuguese had been the first to appear in force in the Indies, other Europeans hastened to join them. Two of Magellan's ships, the *Victoria* and *Trinidad,* touched on their way around the world at Kalimantan and Maluku after the commander's death in the Philippines.

This started an international argument about rights in the Far East. The Pope had made his famous division of the world between Spain and Portugal, and the Portuguese claimed the Indies were all theirs. So the Spanish, hoping to establish their claim, sent a seven-ship fleet the long way around the world—across the Atlantic, around South America, and across the Pacific. Cortez sent an additional group of three ships from his base in Mexico. Only one ship from each group reached the Indies. But in 1571 the Spanish had completed conquest of the nearby Philippines. They were well established there by the time Portuguese power was fading in Maluku.

Spain won some posts in Maluku, but never became strong elsewhere in Indonesia. However, the ebb and flow of Spanish naval and commercial rivalry with other Europeans at home had a strong effect on the history of the Indies.

Britain and Holland also followed the Portuguese toward the magnet of the Spice Islands. Sir Francis Drake, one of the most famous of British sailors, visited Indonesian waters before the days of his highest glory. He was followed by other Englishmen. British trade developed actively and much later there was a moment of British political power in the islands. But it was the British defeat of the Spanish Armada in 1588 that played a larger part than any British action in the archipelago itself. With Spanish naval power cut down, the saucy ships of the Dutch could sail the seas with less worry about their former masters.

The way to the Indies was no secret by the end of the sixteenth century. Long before Jamestown and Plymouth had ever seen a white man, Vasco da Gama's route around Africa and Magellan's around South America were well known to Europeans. Ships from various countries had been to the Indies and back, and there was even a kind of guidebook by a Dutchman, Van Linschoten, who had traveled with the Portuguese in the East.

Nowhere was Van Linschoten's book read with more interest than in the seafaring communities of Holland. The first Dutch

expedition of four ships left for the Indies in 1595. In the following
year they visited Sumatra, Java, and Bali. The next expedition included eight ships, and in the following five years sixty-five vessels
made the voyage.

First contacts between the Portuguese and the Dutch were not
unfriendly, only suspiciously courteous. But the Portuguese were not
keen on sharing the rich prize of the Indies with later arrivals from
Europe. A trade war could be foreseen.

A Portuguese war fleet based on Goa and Malacca was ordered
to sweep Dutch vessels from the Indian Ocean. But the temptation
to attack and plunder other ships as well became too strong to resist.
The Portuguese came to regard any vessel as their prey, including
the ships of the Javanese kingdoms.

The Javanese struck back. They crippled the Portuguese fleet
so badly that it was unable to stop the next Dutch expedition when
it arrived. And at the very time when Spanish-Portuguese reinforcements might have been sent to help drive the Dutch away, the
British on the other side of the world were blockading the port of
Lisbon. Portugal's day as a power in the Indies was finished, and the
future belonged to the Dutch and British, even though Portugal
managed to hang on to Malacca for forty years more and to the
eastern half of Timor until 1976.

The Indonesians thought of the Dutch as allies against Portugal. In any event they liked the chance to play Europeans off against
each other in competition for the spices and other articles of trade.
If they could have seen into the future, they would have been less
enthusiastic. The Dutch were to gain a spice-trade monopoly far
tighter than the Portuguese had ever dreamed of, and it was often
accompanied by cruel hardship for Maluku people. The Dutch had
started on the road to control of the Indies as a whole.

It must be said, however, that from the first appearance of the
Dutch they were often aided and encouraged by local kings. Many
of the local rulers were playing the Dutch game for their own reasons

of profit, or to keep up royal dignity, or as part of a power play against a rival kingdom. There was nothing improper in this according to the terms of the day, even though the welfare of the common people had no part in their thinking. The same pattern of colonial history is to be found in many other parts of the world.

Whenever we Americans feel inclined to adopt a high moral tone about seventeenth-century events on the opposite side of the world, we should think of examples a little later but much closer to home. The record of the dealings of the white man with the Native Americans in the eighteenth and nineteenth centuries leaves little room for indignation against the Dutch at that time, or against local kings who made unwise treaties against their people's interest.

In the rivalry in the East, the Catholic powers of Spain and Portugal were the military enemies opposed by the Protestant Dutch and the Protestant British. But the struggle of lasting importance in the Indies was between these Dutch and British. Or rather, it was between the Dutch East India Company and the British East India Company, both formed to profit from the Indies trade. The two companies were started at about the same time, around 1600.

While the Dutch were starting their empire in the Spice Islands, the British concentrated at first in the western part of the Indies. They opened trade relations with Aceh in northern Sumatra and other pepper producers, and also with Banten, the kingdom at the western end of Java where the Dutch also were doing business. But the riches of the Spice Islands continued to beckon. The British decided they would like to share in the profitable business of buying cloves, nutmeg, and mace (a byproduct made from the nutmeg pod) at low prices in the Indies and selling at fantastic profit in Europe.

England succeeded in taking two small islands in Maluku in 1616 (the year of Shakespeare's death), even while expanding their operations in Sumatra and Java. Then, two years later, they sent a fleet of six ships under Thomas Dale, who had just returned from service as deputy governor of Virginia. Dale nearly captured the

Dutch fortified post on Java that was later to become the most famous city in Indonesia. This was Sunda Kalapa, or Jacatra. Later it was to be renamed Batavia by the Dutch and Jakarta by the Indonesians.

Like British and French generals in North America who had frequent trouble with the Indian tribes allied with them, Dale's dispute with his Indonesian allies cost him dearly. While he and the Indonesian chiefs were arguing about the method of taking what looked like the certain surrender, Dutch reinforcements arrived. The British lost not only Jacatra but, somewhat later, their fleet as well.

Back at home, King James I of England had persuaded the British East India Company to make a treaty with the Dutch company. Each was to supply warships for opposing the Spanish and

Cacao pods, whose seeds give cocoa and chocolate. These seeds were among the many products that were brought by English and Dutch trading companies and sold at a great profit in Europe.

Portuguese, and they were to share both the cost of forts and the spice and pepper trade.

The British company did not really want this plan arranged by their king. They were not keen on fighting in the Far East. Their aim was entirely commercial. The Dutch, though no less eager for profits, wanted to drive all competitors from the area. The partnership did not work, and the British effort at keeping on by themselves had little success. Some British trading posts were continued, but most of their activity was now shifted to India and the New World.

It is interesting for Americans to note that not many years separated two Dutch-British transactions on two sides of the world. Peter Stuyvesant, by surrendering to the British in New York, ended the threat of Dutch competition on the American continent in 1664. And in 1682 the British gave up Banten, their last important post in the Indies, leaving practically a clear field for the Dutch.

Little by little through the seventeenth century the Dutch gained control over more places in the islands. Sometimes they backed a local king against a rival, sometimes they conquered on their own, sometimes they made trade agreements, but always they kept inching out into wider areas. The British were to have a brief comeback of political power as a distant result of the American Revolution and Napoleonic Wars a century later, and the northern part of Kalimantan was destined to come into their sphere. Also, until 1976, the Portuguese continued to hold the eastern half of the island of Timor in the extreme southeast. But with those exceptions, Indonesia was to be a Dutch domain for more than two and a half centuries—until the time of the Japanese invasion in 1942 during World War II.

5

Empire of the Dutch

The golden age of the Netherlands was the seventeenth century. The name is justified by the richness of Dutch cultural life, the glory of its painters such as Rembrandt, and the wisdom of its scholarly humanists and scientists. But it was also a golden time of material wealth.

That wealth was created by the little band of Dutchmen in Batavia and other Indonesian ports on the other side of the world. They were building an empire that was to become almost sixty times the area of the home country, and which was for centuries the mainstay of Holland's economy.

Eventually they settled into Indonesia so well that they came to think of it as belonging to them instead of the Indonesians, who outnumbered them in the islands 250 to 1. Unlike British colonials who spent their working lives in Asia but dreamed of plum pudding and shady lanes and British countryside at home, many of the Dutch felt that Indonesia *was* home. When Indonesia won its freedom, some of the Dutch families had lived in the Indies for a century or so longer than the oldest Anglo-Saxon American family has yet lived west of the Mississippi. Many a Dutchman would tell you with pride that he was born in Batavia or Bandung or Surabaya, and with the same hometown enthusiasm of someone from Amsterdam or The Hague. Bitterness at having lost "his" country to the Indonesians in the twentieth century was made more understandable by the touching sentiment of memories.

But when we look at Dutch control of the Indies from the Indonesian point of view, how different the picture! For much of the time until the twentieth century, and in some ways even until Dutch power ended in the islands, profit for Holland was the main concern. The welfare of the Indonesian people did not seem to matter. It is to the credit of honest Dutch historians that these facts are clearly shown in their own records. And it is to the credit of Dutch humanitarians that they brought the evils to light and worked for reform.

Some reforms came, but only very slowly. Little was done to help the individual Indonesian stand on his own feet in human dignity. The Dutch were so absorbed in material progress that they seemed to forget that it is true for Indonesians, quite as much as for Europeans or any other people, that man does not live by bread alone.

The Dutch correctly say that cruelty and tyranny were already in the Indies in homegrown varieties long before Europeans arrived. They merely used existing customs and the oppressive feudal system for their own purposes. Holland's indirect rule through the princes and village headmen, using the old system of oppression and often deliberately strengthening it, seemed to be succeeding. That prevented the Dutch from seeing until too late the great changes going on in Indonesian thought. The new ideas and new spirit burst out, when the time came, in political revolution. But the people had not been prepared, either by education or by going through the steps of self-government, for the heavy task of running their own affairs.

We will return to this question of independence in another chapter. But first let us follow the steps by which the empire of the Netherlands East Indies was created.

Between 1618 and 1621 the Dutch fortified their storehouse at

Jacatra, changed the name to Batavia, and turned back the British
attempt at taking it from them. That may be regarded as the true
start of the empire of the Dutch East India Company, in spite of
the earlier activities. The Dutch went on expanding the field of their
operations and pouring a golden stream of profits into the home
country.

In 1641 they took Malacca from the Portuguese and defeated
Sultan Agung of Mataram, who had besieged Batavia. In the 1660s
they curbed the wild independence of the kingdom of Aceh in
northern Sumatra (not permanently, however, as the Acehnese
made noisy and colorful re-entries into the Indonesian drama every
few decades). The last Spanish post was eliminated from Maluku,
and the powerful kingdoms of Ternate, Tidore, and Makassar were
all brought into line.

Shortly after that, the strongest monarchy in Java, that of
Mataram, acknowledged the sovereignty of the Dutch. The other
leading kingdom in Java, Banten, just west of Batavia, was likewise
subdued. Through most of the seventeenth century, even after the
Netherlands stopped being a great power in Europe, the Dutch
position in the Indies was continually strengthened.

Toward the end of the eighteenth century, however, real troubles came as a result of foreign events, though things had been going
along fairly well in the Indies themselves. The Dutch had taken a
hand in the three long wars of the Java Succession (fights about who
would sit on a vacant throne). By the end of the third war, just past
mid-century, Batavia rather than any Javanese kingdom was for
the first time the major power on the island of Java. The Dutch
could—and did—appoint and depose kings at will. Things looked
fine from Holland's point of view. But misfortunes began to pile up
a few decades later, at the time of the American Revolution, when
the British blockaded Dutch ports and frequently captured Dutch
vessels.

With shipping stopped, unsold goods piled up in the Batavia warehouses, and for a period of about thirty years the colony often seemed on the edge of bankruptcy. It was left pretty much to itself, with little help from home and also without nearly as much direct control as in the past.

When the British fleet stopped the Dutch from carrying goods to Europe, Batavia welcomed the ships of other countries. They made their purchases on the spot and took them home at their own risk. Both Danish and American vessels came often during this period.

But the French Revolution and Napoleonic Wars brought still greater trouble. France conquered the Netherlands in 1795 and upset the old ruling group. A few years later the Dutch East India Company was dissolved, and control of its business was taken over by the new government in Holland. Even before that, however, the British had soundly beaten the company's war fleet in Indies waters.

In 1796 nearly all Dutch territory except Java and the eastern islands was lost to the British. It was given back under the Treaty of Amiens, but within a year yet another war broke out, and once more the Dutch lost most of the islands.

Napoleon put his brother Louis Bonaparte on the throne of Holland, and in 1810 formally annexed the country. So the Indies became French territory for a time. If the common man in Indonesia had been aware of what was happening on the world stage, he would surely have felt like a volleyball, being batted back and forth from one country to the other.

The British knew that the colony was weakly defended, and that Napoleon could not send much help to that far corner of his empire. So they moved in with great force, and this time even Java fell to them.

The director of the British attack was the great Lord Minto, Governor-General of India. He was a farsighted imperialist. But he is best remembered in the Far East not for himself but for his brilliant assistant, Thomas S. Raffles, known later as the father of modern Singapore.

Raffles ruled the Indies for more than four years, beginning in 1811. His new idea of colonial government and his deep interest in the life and culture of the Indonesians had influence on later history. Not much was actually achieved during Raffles's own time, but as we look back we see that ideas were planted for the future.

Dutch colonials had always dealt with the princes and nobility. Usually they ignored the culture, religion, and way of life of the people upon whose labor the profit for Europeans depended. Both Raffles and his chief, Lord Minto, however, saw the practical as well as humane need to think of human welfare. Also, they had real curiosity about the history and method of living of these people over whose destiny God (with great wisdom, in their judgment) had placed them. They surrounded themselves with expert students of Indonesian culture and affairs. Raffles himself later wrote a remarkable *History of Java*.

Raffles was ambitious, conceited, stubborn, and tricky. Later he was an intriguer against Dutch-British peace, and some people feel he came close to treason in defying his own government. It is a fact, however, that Raffles was the first European in high authority to put the common people of Indonesia where they belonged—in the center of the picture. For that he deserves an honored place in the country's history, even though he had not done much except make a clean break with the past by the time Indonesia was turned back to the Dutch once more in 1816, after the Congress of Vienna.

Perhaps Raffles's scheme would not have worked anyway, even if he had been given more time, but there was soundness in some of the ideas. He felt that the previous system of "forced deliveries" of produce, imposed on the people through the princes, would not work for the long term. The Dutch officials required a fixed amount of rice or pepper or coffee at fixed prices, and this merely made the princes grind down the peasants. The people doing the real work thus had no stake in the operation and no urge to improve production. Raffles's new plan was based on the theory that a large part of the land belonged to the Europeans in Batavia and could be rented to the peasants, who would thus deal directly with Batavia, rather than with the idle and socially useless kings.

But the village chiefs made the deals with the peasants under this "land rent" system, and they often misused their power as badly as the princes had in the past. There were also other faults in the plan. But it pointed the way toward a more modern economic system and, many years later, the complete end of feudalism. It helped human welfare very little in actual practice and had nothing to do with humanitarian ideas, according to Raffles's many Dutch critics. But it did break entirely new ground in one way. It at least *stated* that the well-being of the common people should be a main objective of colonial management.

About a dozen years after the Dutch had taken back their colony from Raffles came one of the greatest shifts in economic life. This was the "Culture System." Sweeping changes resulted. Under this policy the Indies became, in effect, a huge Dutch plantation, organized and run by the Batavia government. Not only was there more direct control of the individual Indonesian, but the Dutch had a far more active part in the operations. They took charge of selecting crops and deciding how to raise them; they conducted wide research and built engineering works such as the big systems of irrigation.

Before then the Dutch had been chiefly traders, buying produce that the Indonesians were forced to bring to them. Now they were becoming active planters, operating the biggest farm in the world. At an earlier period in Maluku they had tried to control production of cloves and nutmeg. But elsewhere, and especially in Batavia, before the Culture System the Dutch had been running trading posts in some ways like those of the Hudson's Bay Company in Canada, or like Bent's Fort and other posts of the Yankee fur traders in the American West.

The Culture System's emphasis on single crops for each area brought serious economic, social, and even nutritional problems. The crops for external markets brought profit all right, but at the expense of food crops. And the profit went to the Netherlands rather than being used for the welfare of the people who produced the crops. The new method was economically successful in short-run terms. And it brought exciting advances to Indonesian agriculture. The long-suffering peasant, however, had merely gained rule by a foreign country in exchange for the old rule by his own princes. Actually, he was worse off than before, because Dutch control of his life as a farmer did not end the other kinds of tyranny from which he suffered. The king and the village chief kept great power, and this power was sustained by the Dutch as long as it helped or at least did not interfere with their operations.

Real harm was done to the local "village council," which was a kind of basic democracy. These councils reached decisions by consensus, postponing any action until all agreed on a compromise. The headman had been more a spokesman for the group than ruler of the village. But under the Culture System, the headman became a virtual dictator because of the power given to him by the Dutch.

Some people think that this injury to grass-roots democracy may be partly to blame for some of Indonesia's later troubles. They think that if the village councils had been encouraged they might have laid the ground for a national government, in the same way that New England town meetings gave a base for our republic. In any event, the Culture System failed to free the peasant, and it stored up hatreds that appeared in the form of Communism and revolution a century later.

The area under actual Dutch control was greatly enlarged under the Culture System. Or, rather, an actual *area* was now controlled, instead of a few isolated points as in the past. The growth resulted from the new vision of wider inland crop-planting instead of relying on trading posts and areas close to the ports.

But it was also a countermove to a swashbuckling British adventurer, James Brooke, later called "the white rajah of Sarawak." In the 1840s he took the northern edge of the island of Kalimantan, consisting of the three territories now called Brunei, Sarawak, and Sabah, the last two of which became part of Malaysia.

Brooke's Hollywood-style empire-building on one of their own islands made the Dutch see that it was high time to confirm their own claims. So in the next fifteen years, inspired both by the British threat and by the chance for profit from new crops, the Netherlands Indies expanded to about the size of the present Indonesian Republic.

During the middle years of the nineteenth century, Dutch reformers began to protest against unfair and brutal treatment of Indonesians, especially during forceful "pacifications" in areas newly taken over. From this time on, the government was under constant attack from at least part of Dutch public opinion. The officials were accused of breaking treaties, permitting slavery and promoting the opium trade, draining the islands of their wealth without equal benefits to Indonesia, and of treating the people like second-class citizens in their own country. And there was special criticism of the neglect of the educational needs of the people who were Holland's wards.

Just as *Uncle Tom's Cabin* stirred American hearts against slavery in this country, a famous Dutch book, *Max Havelaar*, aroused opinion about Holland's policy in the Indies. The author, Douwes Dekker, who wrote under the pen name of "Multatuli," was himself a former colonial official, and he had seen things firsthand. So had W. R. Van Hoevell, a clergyman who became a strong pleader for more generous and humane treatment after he had been expelled from the Indies for saying the same things there.

People like Dekker, Van Hoevell, and others were supported by a rising tide of European liberalism, and as a result of all these pressures certain reforms were carried out. Slavery was forbidden in 1860, three years before Lincoln's Emancipation Proclamation. Improvements were made in legal justice. The cruder forms of cheating Indonesians in business deals were forbidden in theory and to some extent actually ended. But the reform that had the most lasting effect was the law stopping non-Indonesians from buying land.

In keeping with liberal ideas at the time, there was a movement of private business into the Indies, and a big immigration from the home country. At first the officials in Batavia had tried to aid their treasury by selling land. There was real danger that, if the policy had kept on, foreign capitalists would have gotten control not only of the business of the islands but of all the land as well. Ownership would have gone into fewer and fewer hands, making a class of great landowners, and thus leading to the "landlord problem" that still troubles many other parts of Asia.

A minor footnote to this is of American interest. The town of Holland, Michigan, owes its existence to the rule about land purchase in Indonesia. A clergyman, Albertus Van Raalte, and a group of his religious followers in Holland had planned founding a colony in Java. When they were ready to leave they learned that they would be forbidden to buy land in Java (though they were offered some in Maluku), so they went to America instead. In 1847 they founded the Michigan town that bears the name of their home country and is famous for its tulips.

There were many swings backward and forward through Indonesian history about whether the government should take part in business. The Culture System was merely the most dramatic step. Control of spice production in Maluku had ended soon after Raffles's defeat. The Culture System put the Batavia officials heavily back into business again, especially with coffee and sugar. It was not until the last third of the nineteenth century that private business began taking over from the officials, and for one crop, coffee, the Culture System did not end until 1917.

The last big change in relations of Holland with its colony came at the start of the present century with the so-called "Ethical Policy." This reflected both the humane influence of reform and a growing feeling among Dutch businessmen that a prosperous Indies could be a wonderful market for what they had to sell. It was also thought that taxes on private business in the Indies would help carry the cost of running the colony. This had become a heavy drain on the home country.

For the Indonesian people the great gain from the Ethical Policy was the new approach to education, public health, and other help to the public welfare. Nationalists later said that these measures were too little and too late, but they did represent a big change from the former official attitude. And some of the Dutch officials in this period, especially some of the teachers and doctors, were as devoted in trying to serve the Indonesians as if they had been working for their own people. They could not get the Government to provide the sums they saw were needed, but they themselves did their best.

We know far too little about the life of the common people in Indonesia before the twentieth century. Most of the earlier Western contact was with princes and other highborn people. Few of the Dutch in the Indies studied the lives of ordinary people until quite late in the colonial period.

Before the Culture System, the colonial managers were so out of touch with people away from the ports and palaces that one writer guesses that before 1800 the great majority of Indonesians had never seen a white man. A Dutch governor in the seventeenth century boasted that for twenty-five years he had ruled the Indies from his castle in Batavia without ever leaving the town except for one or two hunting expeditions in the jungle nearby. Other stories show that nearly two centuries later many of the Dutch still had little interest in Indonesians or their way of life. Too often there was ignorance of the rich cultural heritage, narrow-mindedness about the religion, and full certainty that the people were naturally lazy and incapable of education.

The Indonesians' own history does not help us very much, either. It deals largely with royalty and the nobility, and much of the time merely reports fanciful events, retelling Hindu-Javanese legends in a new setting.

In spite of the lack of full historical sources, we know that control from above had become the natural way of life, whether the ruler was a local sultan, the Dutch East India Company, the Dutch government, or a private corporation. That was a poor background for national independence, let alone democratic life needing a body of self-reliant citizens. It goes far toward explaining many of the troubles the Indonesians had after winning independence.

6

Nature's Bounty with Man's Help

Whatever judgment history may give about Dutch control of the *people* in the Indies, there can be no question about the wonder, the green miracle, of what they did with nature at the same time. Especially during the period of the Culture System and later, they found new crops and new ways to increase productivity. They also found new mineral deposits and developed ingenious systems of irrigation, transport, and communication.

When Europeans first came to the Indies, their frantic interest in quick profits from spices made them overlook a greater prize right under their noses. It was like the fevered gold rush in California in 1849, with little thought at that time of California's far greater and continuing wealth in cotton, wheat, oranges, and so on.

For more than a century after their arrival, the Europeans ignored the potential wealth of Java, which since then has become one of the most richly productive spots in the entire world. And the cloves and nutmeg that once seemed like the greatest treasure of the East are now so unimportant in the full picture of Indonesian wealth that we think of them chiefly as part of the closed book of history.

As a matter of fact, the story of the spices in Maluku shows the problems people run into when trying to control production. At the

47

time when cloves and nutmeg could be found nowhere else in the world, the Dutch not only established their monopoly but set about destroying unwanted trees whose produce might have gone onto the market via smugglers, or at least might have lowered the market price by making the spices too plentiful. British, Portuguese, and sometimes American traders were using Makassar, the future Ujung Pandang, as their base, and for a time the smugglers from Maluku were busy supplying them.

Destruction of the clove and nutmeg trees in Maluku was a tragedy for the people living on those islands. One Dutch historian speaks of the people as having been "exterminated" during the forcible conquest, and at all events the natural means of livelihood of many of them was taken away. This control of production (like acreage control and plowing-under in our country at a later day) did keep the price up for a while.

But it would have seemed like poetic justice to the people of Maluku if they had known that the policy cost the Dutch dearly later on. World demand for the spices increased, but there were no more trees upon which the Dutch could draw. Although clove and nutmeg trees bear fruit for decades, the first crop does not come for ten or a dozen years after planting. So it was impossible for the Dutch in Maluku to overcome the shortage soon enough to take advantage of the good market.

In the meantime both the British and French had managed to smuggle saplings into their own colonies. Today, most of the world's cloves come not from Indonesia, but from the islands of Zanzibar and Madagascar, and the biggest nutmeg production is in the British West Indies and Brazil. It is not surprising that after that experience the Dutch decided, in the first quarter of the nineteenth century, that freer trade in spices, without either forced deliveries or restricted production, would be to their advantage.

Forced deliveries were still the rule elsewhere, however, for instance pepper from Banten and rice from Mataram, the two kingdoms on either side of the main trading base of Batavia. This method of doing business kept on in large degree until the start of the Culture System. In effect, Batavia said to a local king: "We don't care how you do it, but in the next year you must deliver so many tons of pepper, for which we will pay you so much per ton."

The king, wanting the military and financial support of the Dutch, and being prevented by them from trading with anyone else, passed on the orders to his subjects. They were given little help or advice, but simply told the quantity needed. The king, thereupon, returned to his life of pleasures and ceremonies and useless local wars.

At the beginning of the eighteenth century the crops were those that had been customary for many years. Rice was the chief food, and pepper, spices, and sugar brought the largest income. But a spirit of experiment took hold of a few Dutchmen in the Indies, and new ideas were tried out.

Coffee was the first big success. Plants were given to district chiefs near Batavia, and a hundred pounds of coffee beans were produced in 1711. The amount grew and grew, to more than 10 million pounds per year a decade later. Coffee was Indonesia's chief export crop in the last quarter of the century, and the American slang expression "a cup of java" reminds us of the time when Yankee sailors in the Pacific thought of Batavia as the natural source of the world's coffee.

Coffee was the only big new crop before the Culture System led to wholesale research and experiment. When it did, however, great events followed one after the other. The Botanical Gardens at Bogor, not far from Batavia, became a center of agricultural research. Scientists in many parts of the islands were tireless in trying new plants and new ways of growing them.

Tobacco had come from America via the Spanish in the seventeenth century, and at least some tobacco was grown from that time on. But it remained for a private company in the nineteenth century

Lily pads (seven feet wide) in the Botanical Gardens at Bogor

to learn how the plant would thrive in cleared jungle districts of northern Sumatra, and how it would respond to the highly scientific method of culture that was adopted. Special types grow in Sumatra, Java, and Madura, each being prized for qualities not found in most other tobaccos.

The oil palm of West Africa was an import to Indonesia in the middle of the nineteenth century, and it proved to be successful almost from the start. Two kinds of oil come from the fruit: palm oil from the pulp, and palm-kernel oil from the pit. The latter is more edible, and is used for making margarine as well as for other purposes. The major use of palm oil is for making soap and candles.

Another picturesque import was the cinchona tree, which came from South America. The new tree took to Indonesian life so well that Java gained more and more of the world market until about 90 percent of the world's supply of medical quinine (used in treating fever) came from the bark of Indonesian trees. Sales have gone way down in recent years, however, because of use of chemical substitutes.

Kapok, the so-called silk-cotton tree, is another immigrant, probably from South America. The "cotton," which comes from the inside of the seed pod, is wonderfully useful because of its light weight and because it resists water. This makes it popular not only for upholstery, pillows, and sleeping bags, but also for life jackets. The tree has prospered in other parts of Asia, but nowhere as well as in Indonesia, which became the chief supplier to the entire world.

Rubber was the most important of all the new cash crops brought in by the Culture System, although results were so long delayed that it was not until about the time of World War I that rubber came into its own in Indonesia. Before that there had been hit-or-miss gathering of the juice from wild rubber trees in Sumatra. After new Brazilian varieties came in via the Botanical Gardens at Bogor, and after development of the plantation method of production, Indonesia gained its position as the largest producer of natural rubber in the world. In 1959 it fell behind Malaya for the first time, and synthetic rubber now makes the prospect for natural rubber less attractive.

Processing rubber in a plant in Java

Sugarcane, an old inhabitant, responded to new plantation methods, and both the yield and the profits increased greatly. Besides rubber and sugar, other crops most frequently produced on plantations are coffee, tea, tobacco, palm oil, cinchona, cacao (whose beans give us cocoa and chocolate, and whose presence in the Netherlands Indies no doubt led to the fame of Dutch chocolate candy), and sisal for rope and twine.

Some of the important cash crops have stayed in the hands of small farmers from the beginning to the present day. Pepper gardens, which are found most often in Sumatra, are usually small, and frequently are an informal addition to other kinds of work—like the raising of turkeys or sunflower seeds for "pin money" by an American farmer's wife. Indonesia was the largest supplier of pepper until World War II, when India gained first place.

After several failures, tea from the Assam province of India was found to be adaptable to Java. A tea garden must have just the right combination of warm temperature, generous rain, and proper altitude, and these conditions are found on Javanese mountainsides. Tea gardens are a most attractive feature of the landscape, and Indonesia became for many years the third largest tea producer in the world.

Coconut production is still almost entirely in the hands of small owners. The product is used in many ways at home and is exported for a variety of purposes to the rest of the world. The export is made in the form of coconut oil or of copra (dried coconut meat). As with so many other crops, production fell off badly during World War II and the aftermath, but Indonesia could still be the world's largest source of coconut oil for soap, margarine, and glycerine, not to mention minor byproducts of the tree. These include oil cake, a stock feed made from what is left of the meat after the oil has been pressed out; coir, a fiber made from the husk and used for cordage and matting; and shredded coconut for cakes and candy bars.

Even the crops used entirely for home consumption rather than

A Javanese tea garden

cash sale, and grown entirely by families instead of plantation companies, gained from the scientific advance. The best example is the cassava, a root plant that is even more generous than the potato in producing edible starch. We meet it on our own table in the form of tapioca. The plant had been introduced by the Spanish and Portuguese in the seventeenth century, but better varieties were brought in from Latin America by the nineteenth-century scientists. The cassava became, and has continued to be, a food source following only rice and corn as the staff of life for Indonesians.

At first the technicians thought of the forests as their enemy, because crop land was what they were seeking, and the clearing of jungles was a back-breaking job. But before long the wealth of the forests came to interest them greatly, especially because a large part of all the land area of Indonesia is forested. Many of Indonesia's timber and forest products are used locally, but exports include teakwood, rattan (a climbing palm that, when cut into strips, is a major source of chair seats and wickerwork), bamboo, camphor, barks for tanning leather, and delightfully scented woods whose oil for making perfumes was one of the prized exports to Europe in the early days. Timber has come to follow directly after oil and gas in the list of export commodities according to value. But the need for reforestation, which has been so familiar to us for a long time, is now troubling the Indonesians because of the "timber rush" that has removed so many trees. Leaching and soil erosion have troubled many areas where trees have been lost.

Fisheries also received attention in the scientific revolution, not only studies of the habits of mackerel, tuna, sardines, anchovies, and other fish living in the ocean, but also the stocking of lakes and inland streams, and the development of fish culture in ponds and in the paddies between rice crops.

While some scientists were working along all these lines, geologists, oil drillers, and mining engineers were exploring the mineral riches beneath the earth. Of the products found in this way, petroleum seemed the most important. In recent years it has represented over 65 percent of the value of Indonesia's total exports. However in world terms Indonesian oil is not a major factor, only about 2 percent of the total. Oil production has increased substantially in recent years and may go even higher. But domestic use is taking an increasing share of the total produced, so it is believed that Indonesia might stop being a net exporter. On the other hand, natural gas has become a major export commodity, and it has been predicted that by 1990 liquefied natural gas (LNG) may replace oil as Indonesia's biggest source of foreign exchange. Indonesia has large coal reserves and there are good possibilities for thermal energy (especially heat from volcanoes). Those two sources may ease the need for drawing on petroleum for local use.

Tin had been mined to some extent for centuries, but both its use and ways of getting more of it increased greatly during the age of science. The three small Indonesian islands of Bangka, Billiton, and Singkep, between Sumatra and Kalimantan, have rich deposits. They gave the country second place in the world for amount of tin ore brought out of the ground. And Indonesia is believed to have a sixth of all the unmined tin in the world. Bauxite (the one from which we get aluminum) is produced, and nickel also ranks high on the list of future economic prospects. The production of salt, manganese, iodine, and limestone is active, and there is a modest continuing production of the two metals that brought Indian seafarers in the first place—gold and silver. Copper mining is quite new, but an American company has a mine in production in Irian Jaya.

But of all the benefits to Indonesia through the work of scientists, engineers, farm organizers, and managers, perhaps none had more effect on the people than the elaborate irrigation systems. Existing Indonesian systems were improved, and great new ones were designed and built by the Dutch. Especially in Java, these enlarged the area that would bear crops and multiplied the yield per acre of land already farmed. Increase in the total food supply in this and all the other ways permitted a growth in population seeming to defy all the rules of natural limitation.

The island of Java, with its small companion, Madura, had a population of about 5 million a century and a half ago. Today the same area supports—and not badly by Asian standards—about 95 million. There are signs that a limit has been reached. And there have been other reasons besides Java's crops for the island's prosperity. Sumatrans, for instance, say that their wealth and that of other Outer Islands has helped to support the Javanese. They have complained that Java has taken too large a share of the money income from foreign sales of oil and rubber produced on the Outer Islands. That is a good point. But the overflowing productivity of Java is still one of the miracles of man's use of nature's bounty.

All in all, the new approach that the Dutch brought to Indonesia's natural resources not only gave handsome returns to the foreign capitalists but also built a "capital plant" that is one of the most remarkable on the face of the earth. Why, then, did the Indonesians want to escape from Dutch management of their affairs? That is another and quite different story, which we will come to in the next chapter.

7

On the Road to

Independence

When Indonesia declared itself to be a free country in 1945, it had passed a historic milestone on a long, hard road. The road stretched back many years, and to travel it called for heroism and steadfast courage from many people. That milestone, however, was also the start of a much harder path, along which Indonesia is still going. That was the effort at creating a new country and of leading it to a place of honor and dignity among the nations of the world.

We cannot say too often that it seems almost a miracle that there is a Republic of Indonesia at all, so great were the dangers that threatened it on every hand at birth, and so baffling the problems faced after independence. But the Indonesians themselves were not content with mere nationhood. They wanted their country to serve the welfare of all its people, and at the same time to accept its duty as a great free nation in the modern world.

To understand that high challenge, we need to know something of how independence came about, and of how perilously close to failure it has been at many points along the way.

Through the centuries there had been anti-Portuguese, anti-British, anti-Dutch activity; nowadays these actions might be called anti-imperialist or anti-colonial. Although there were occasional popular uprisings, for the most part they had little to do with personal freedom for Indonesians. Usually a local king was trying to get the upper hand over a rival who was allied with one of the foreign powers from Europe. Those were kings' wars rather than people's wars. Some of them, however, deserve notice in any record of the movement to throw off foreign control.

During the seventeenth century, the Sultan Abulfatah of Banten, with great energy and cleverness, built a shipping fleet of his own and carried on lively foreign trade with the Philippines, India, and even Persia. He sent ambassadors to other Indonesian kingdoms as far away as Maluku, and he invited both England and Turkey to become his allies.

Abulfatah was finally captured by the Dutch and the power of Banten was destroyed. But a little later a former slave from Bali, named Surapati, caused even more trouble. He was regarded at first as a mere bandit, but he set up an area of his own in East Java. He was joined there by a man familiarly called Sunan Mas, only son of the recently deceased sultan of Mataram. The young sultan held strong anti-Dutch views, so Batavia decided to remove him from the throne. Their troops did that, putting a more manageable relative in his place.

Sunan Mas and Surapati together assembled quite a force in their East Java stronghold. The Dutch had to carry out a long hard campaign before Surapati was killed and Sunan Mas was captured and sent into exile. Surapati was no saint, and in many ways he makes poor material for a national hero. His murder of Dutch ambassadors was painfully like the treachery of Europeans under flags of truce on other occasions. But there was a spirit of "Indonesia for the Indonesians" in his rebellion, and he holds a place among the earlier fighters for freedom.

An even more dramatic rising of Indonesians against the foreigners was led by Diponegoro in the nineteenth century, and it was the biggest until the final struggle. Diponegoro's name is borne today by one of the handsome streets in Jakarta, and he is regarded as a freedom fighter who was a century ahead of his time.

Diponegoro was the rightful heir to a throne, and was supposed to be Sultan of Yogyakarta. But Batavia had decided the title should go to a younger brother who they felt was more likely to do their bidding. During the rebellion Diponegoro proved himself to be a cunning guerrilla fighter, and an effective rouser of the people. But he was also a mystic, and that was part of his popular appeal. After he was driven from his throne he spent some time in Hindulike meditation as a hermit, living in caves and wandering through the countryside. He had wide support from the peasants, who told miraculous stories about him, some of them apparently borrowed from the eleventh-century legends of King Airlangga. Before the end many of the aristocrats sided with him also.

For five years Diponegoro carried on his guerrilla war. It was a tragic campaign in which deaths from cholera and famine were far more numerous than those on the battlefield. Diponegoro must have been a careless reader of the history of the Indies if he was surprised at what happened when he finally accepted a Dutch invitation to come to their camp to talk about surrender. He was promptly arrested and sent into exile!

The Diponegoro revolt began over a familiar dispute about a throne, but it grew into a popular struggle. It was a real predecessor of later fights for freedom, in that sense perhaps like Bacon's Rebellion in Virginia a century before the American Revolution.

There were other examples of standing up to the foreigners, in Maluku, Java, and Sulawesi. Some were under the leadership of warrior queens. But special mention must be made of Aceh, where a rugged and unquenchable people live at the northern tip of Sumatra. From the beginning of Indonesian history right to the present day, they have shown a rambunctious spirit that reminds Americans of Texas under the Lone Star flag. No one has been able to keep the Acehnese down for long.

Aceh has had some relatively quiet periods, but it keeps bursting out all over again. Its position on the Strait of Malacca made piracy convenient, and the Acehnese took to it with joy. They resisted the kind of "pacification" that the Dutch found rather easy to apply at other places in the islands. Their longest fight with the Dutch began in 1873 and lasted for over thirty years. Their guerrilla bands were a thorn in the side of the Republic in later years.

As the world moved into the twentieth century, and as profits for foreign investors soared to heights never known before, it became clear that Indonesians would refuse to go on forever with little voice in their own affairs. And it was also clear that if they had a voice they would try to divert more of the profits into education, public health, better living conditions, and other welfare purposes.

In an American study of the income per person in fifty-three countries at the end of the Dutch period, just before World War II, Indonesia was number fifty-three with an average of $22 per year! In a largely agricultural country such as Indonesia it is not easy to keep track of all the income in the form of food both raised and eaten at home. Even so, Indonesia's place at the bottom of the list in spite of the wealth it had given to Holland through the years was deeply resented by the nationalists. And the Communists made full use of the fact in their propaganda.

Most Indonesians had passed the point where they would accept anything less than real self-government. They were bitter against the halfway measures by which they felt the Dutch were putting off the inevitable day when Indonesians would take things into their own hands. The most serious fault of the Dutch in the twentieth century was that, right up to the moment of independence and even afterwards, they were unable to believe that the freedom movement was real. Yet it was growing stronger and had become an effective unifying force among the formerly unrelated ethnic groups and island communities. It was only after settlement of the issue of Irian Jaya in 1963 that relations became both orderly and peaceful.

The national spirit had been growing like a flood that begins with tiny streams in the distant hills, gradually swelling into a mighty river. The officials thought of the nationalists as mere "troublemakers" who could be put down with a strong hand. And they felt that any Dutch who favored self-government for the Indies were little more than traitors. But the spirit of independence was becoming ever stronger. The growing resentment against colonial exploitation was stirred further by events from abroad. The Japanese victory in the Russo-Japanese War in 1905 proved that Asians *could* defeat Westerners. And the earth-shaking Chinese Revolution in 1911 showed how an Asian people could take destiny into their own hands and throw off an outworn system.

Many other strong influences came from abroad. In fact the Indonesian freedom movement seems to have spread out most strongly from just those parts of the country having greatest contact with the outside world. The three biggest influences from abroad, each greatly modified in Indonesia, as was always the case, were a European idea of social justice; the new movement in Islam that tried to combine social and political reform with religion; and international Communism.

One of the first groups contributing to a national spirit in purely Indonesian terms was Budi Utomo ("Lofty Endeavor"), organized in 1908 by three medical students to encourage interest in Javanese culture. One of the three, Sutomo, was an important leader in the freedom movement later on, but the society itself was too intellectual for mass support. It was useful, however, in putting down firm roots for the movement that in other ways drew inspiration from abroad.

Social democracy of the sort known in Europe appealed at first to dissatisfied Dutch and to Eurasians and Chinese. Through them radical social ideas came to the Indies. When the independence movement started, one of the biggest questions was whether freedom and democracy could be gained without falling into the trap of Communism.

Religion was a leading force in preventing the Communists from reaching their goal, which was to capture the national movement. Of a group of Muslim organizations the most important was one called Sarekat Islam, which was strongly influenced by the "modernist" Muslims of the Near East. They had a new vitality in their attitude toward religion, and at the same time they were working for political and social reform. The Sarekat Islam was the extreme eastern end of this movement, and they were determined to keep themselves Islamic, Indonesian, and non-Communist.

Among the leaders of the Sarekat Islam were Haji Oemar Said Cokroaminoto, Haji Samanhudi, and Haji Agus Salim ("haji" indicating that they had made the holy pilgrimage to Mecca). Haji Agus Salim was one of the chief intellectuals of the freedom movement, and later was Foreign Minister of the Republic. In one of the show-down struggles to keep the Communists from controlling the country, the Haji told them they had no monopoly on advanced ideas. He said that Mohammed, the holy prophet of Islam, had been preaching socialist economics twelve centuries before Karl Marx was born!

But although the Communists were turned back from their try at seizing this particular society, they made progress elsewhere. By the middle of the 1920s an underground movement existed, though, oddly enough, at first without much encouragement from Moscow. A Communist uprising in 1926 was against the Kremlin's ideas. Lenin and other Russian leaders had not expected success for Communism in so-called backward countries, and they kept brushing off the eager party organizers in the Indies. Later the Soviets decided they had been wrong, and both they and the Chinese Communists came to think of Indonesia as an important area for their work. The

Communist Party in Indonesia grew enormously in membership and influence after independence.

But the New World played its part also. A high place on the list of foreign influences must be given to the ideas of the Rights of Man that had been expressed by the leaders of the American Revolution and then restated in other ways in the French Revolution.

When the revolutionary French overthrew the ruling group in Holland, and brought in the new ideas of liberty, equality, and fraternity, the colonial officials in Batavia wrote home in some alarm to ask if anything of that sort was intended for the Indies. They were told to relax, that the new doctrine was all right for Europe but naturally not for backward Indonesia.

Dangerous thoughts kept coming in, in spite of Batavia's efforts. Educated Indonesians showed respect for America's Founding Fathers, and especially for people such as Jefferson who gave noble expression to the very thoughts in which they believed.

During the independence movement the national spirit centered in Java, which was the richest island, the most populous, and the most open to ideas from abroad. But both independence and social democracy were ideals on the Outer Islands also, especially in Sumatra. The idea of bringing all the parts together, however, was slow in coming, and many Indonesians as well as the Dutch thought it would never happen. It was curious that two foreign enemies, Holland and Japan, must be credited with helping to bring it about.

The unity of the Dutch system within their colony may have given a geographical base for the Republic of Indonesia. If the Indonesians had been left entirely on their own, without a central Dutch system, it is quite possible that the different islands might have kept on going their separate ways in spite of their general cultural unity.

The Dutch did what they could to prevent *Indonesian* unity, even forbidding, for instance, the use of the word "Indonesia" and from time to time banning use of the growing national language. But they could not do their job as colonial managers without their own kind of unity, which later was taken over by the Indonesians.

But if Holland laid the groundwork, the defeat of the Japanese in World War II fixed the timing. The Japanese invasion of the Indies in 1942 and other events of World War II speeded up the coming of unity and freedom. If it had not been for the Japanese, many Dutch think Holland would have been able to work out some scheme of self-government within a Dutch system like the British Commonwealth. They had started very late, however, and even after the end of World War II their maneuvering cast doubt on their seriousness in accepting a commonwealth plan. Even if the reformers had had a free hand, they might not have been able to make up the time they had let slip while British India and Pakistan, among other colonies, were getting ready for their freedom.

As World War II developed, however, German occupation of Holland beginning in 1940, Japanese occupation of the Indies, and the commitment of all countries in the Atlantic Charter and Declaration by the United Nations made it certain that the old order of things would not be resumed after the war. The great question was whether *some* form of Dutch control would be imposed once more, or whether Indonesia would become entirely free—if, indeed, Communism would not completely smother freedom as well as capitalist imperialism.

At the start of World War II, some of the Indonesian nationalists felt that an Asian alliance of some kind would give them their chance to break the Dutch hold. These people said they had no concern with events in Europe.

Others saw that Hitlerism was a threat to freedom everywhere. They put their faith in the principles of the Atlantic Charter signed by U.S. President Franklin Delano Roosevelt and British Prime Minister Winston Churchill, and later by other countries, including Holland. Even the growing signs that Japan, the major Asian power, would come in on the side of Germany did not stop the Indonesians from supporting the war against Hitler. They were anti-Dutch, but not anti-Allies.

When, even before Pearl Harbor and the American entry into the war, the Japanese began moving south toward the oil, rubber, tin, and foodstuffs of Southeast Asia, it was clear that an invasion was coming. And it was just as clear that the small forces of the Allies would not be able to stop the Japanese. Furthermore, there was an ancient legend that a people with yellow skins would someday come to clear foreign invaders from Indonesian soil.

The invasion came in 1942. The Japanese quickly overran the islands, captured or drove out the Dutch and other Allied forces, and took full control of the Indies. The Japanese immediately pretended to have great enthusiasm for the idea of Indonesian independence. They said they had come to rescue the poor islanders from the cruel

Sukarno, first President of the Republic

rule of Europeans. The Indonesians had true grievances, as we have seen, so the Japanese propaganda had considerable effect. Societies and military units were formed under Japanese sponsorship, with flowery statements of purpose with which an Indonesian patriot would naturally agree.

In spite of that, many Indonesians refused to work with these organizations. But many others did participate, some for selfish reasons, some because they were fooled, and some because they thought it was a way of helping the cause of eventual freedom.

Among the last were two of the most famous Indonesians, Sukarno and Hatta, who later became the first President and Vice-President of the Republic.

These particular collaborators acted deliberately and by agreement among several of the most prominent leaders of the revolution. Some would be outward collaborators with the Japanese, some would run a secret underground movement, and some would take to the hills and organize guerrilla bands in time-honored Indonesian fashion. As in the resistance movements in Europe during the German occupation, the Communists in Indonesia played a full and useful part side by side with anti-Communists for much of the time. The first thing was to get rid of the Japanese, the next was to prevent return of the Dutch, and the last would be to decide what kind of government the new country wanted to have. For the moment, differing long-range views were suppressed.

Little by little it became clear that the Japanese purpose was imperial rule and the placing of Indonesia in a bondage worse than anything the Dutch had ever dreamed of. Although the Japanese were fellow Asians, and even fitted the ancient legend about the yellow-skinned rescuers, disenchantment set in quickly and spread widely. Indonesia realized long before the end of the war that life in a Japanese puppet state would be even less attractive than under the former Dutch rule.

As the end of the war neared, the Japanese tried to make things look better by offering Indonesian "independence," but a strong group of nationalists was opposed to accepting anything as a gift from an invading army. There was a big argument among the leaders, and at one point Sukarno and Hatta were kidnapped to prevent them from putting out a statement disapproved by the others. As so often at other times, students were prime movers in many of the events. At last most of the groups agreed, and Sukarno read Indonesia's own brief declaration of independence on August 17, 1945. Men and women freedom fighters barricaded themselves in radio and telegraph offices to send the message to all parts of the country.

The Republic of Indonesia had begun its career. The question now was whether it could live very long among the many perils that threatened it. The Dutch wanted to get their colony back, the Communists wanted to take control of the revolution for themselves, and nobody knew whether the different regions could really unite into one country.

8

A New World

To declare independence is one thing. Actually to secure it is something very different—as both Americans and Indonesians know from the history of their fights for freedom. President Sukarno's declaration in 1945 was the start of a heroic struggle that was to last more than four years before true independence was won. The victors were not only guerrillas and other soldiers but also students, teachers, scholars, journalists, and diplomats.

The Dutch naturally wanted to go back to running their colony again just as quickly as possible. They thought that America, Britain, and their other allies in the war against Germany and Japan should help them. The Communists, meanwhile, talked independence but actually wanted to rule the country with their party under the leadership of the Soviet Union. And, as if that were not enough enemies for one young republic, Indonesians differed with each other about the future of the new country. Some were true patriots but disagreed about methods. Others were seeking personal power or had some other special interest.

While the Japanese controlled the islands, Indonesian guerrillas and the underground resistance had been planning an uprising, timed for the expected Allied invasion. When word came that the Japanese had given in to the Allies in August 1945, months sooner than had been expected, the Indonesians moved on their own to disarm the troops in the islands.

The Allied high command did not realize the strength of the independence movement. They told the Japanese troops in the Indies to keep their arms, maintain order, and await the arrival of Allied forces before surrendering. This was hard for the Indonesians to understand, after waiting so long. But worse was to come.

British troops came in first. They were welcome enough in themselves. But then Dutch soldiers began arriving, under British protection. The Dutch demanded the arrest of Sukarno and tried to persuade their allies that the so-called independence movement was just a Japanese plot and that the Indonesian leaders were puppets and traitors.

Tragic events followed, and for some months there was heavy fighting, especially in Surabaya, where the Indonesian government was not able to control semiorganized bands, which ran wild. Atrocities were committed by both sides.

After much argument and some action, an Indo-Dutch military truce was signed in November 1946. This was followed by an agreement for a "United States of Indonesia" in which the Republic of Indonesia would be one of the states. The other states in this federal system were Dutch-organized governments from other parts of the islands. According to the Republic people, this was merely a Dutch scheme for the old-time "indirect rule" in new form. In the next few months there were many arguments about how the agreement should be carried out. In July 1947 the Dutch launched a full-scale military attack on the Republic's territory.

Through the good offices of the United Nations this military action was ended in January 1948, but with the Republic's territory reduced to a portion of Java and a little bit of Sumatra. The Republican capital was Yogyakarta, in the middle of Java, and the Dutch held Batavia.

A few months later the Communists chose to start a rebellion within the Republic. The Republic's leaders were busy indeed, putting down the Communist rebels with one hand and trying to hold the Dutch to the agreed truce line with the other.

With the Republic hemmed into its small area, and with the Dutch actively organizing the other parts of the Indies, it looked once more as if the Indonesian nation had reached the end of the road. Discussions about the truce agreement finally came to a deadlock, and in December 1948 Dutch paratroopers fell upon the Republican capital, while troop carriers brought in commandos.

President Sukarno and other top leaders were captured. The chief cities of Java were seized. Still once more it seemed like the final curtain. But the Indonesians would not give in.

Besides Sukarno, the leaders who were led into captivity after they had been seized in Yogyakarta included Hatta, Sjahrir, and Haji Agus Salim. Who were these people, and what were they like? This is perhaps a good time to give a few facts about these men whose hold on the people was so strong that, even in exile, they were the heart of the revolution.

President Sukarno was the leading figure in Indonesian life for more than a quarter of a century, beginning when he was a student. He had a justified reputation as one of the greatest charmers of the modern world. He was always perfectly dressed, carrying an air of strength and "bounce," and with a winning smile. As a public speaker he had an almost mystic power to sway a crowd. He was born to be a master of ceremonies. With zip and energy he accepted any chance to be an organizer, whether of a mass meeting, a songfest, an impromptu folk dance, or a national revolution. Although President of the Republic, he gloried in the name Bung Karno, *bung* meaning brother and being a word used to summon waiters and for other purposes, something like our "Hey, Mac!" It became a symbol of equality during the revolution.

During his longest visit to the United States in 1956 his pleasing personality won friends everywhere. He made a special pilgrimage to Monticello because of his deep admiration for Jefferson. When a collection of Jefferson's writings was published in Indonesian translation some years after that, Sukarno's remarks about Jefferson during his Virginia visit served as the introduction to the book.

Sukarno was educated as an engineer and he is therefore sometimes referred to as Ir. Sukarno, that is, Engineer Sukarno. But his true profession was political leadership. A first name, Achmed, is sometimes used by Westerners who cannot get used to the Indonesian custom of often going by only one name, but to most of his fellow countrymen he was always just Bung Karno.

His enemies said he became a demagogue, a seeker after personal power. His admirers, on the other hand, thought he truly expressed the ideals and hopes of the people. He represented the nation forcefully in a manner that demanded and received international respect. But his following, which at the time of the revolution had included patriots of all kinds, gradually came to lose the intellectual leaders and to depend on mass appeal. Over the years more and more of his one-time supporters became increasingly concerned about Sukarno's acceptance of Communist participation in national affairs. They were also worried about the loss of the country's once open dialogue, and about the more blatant signs of Sukarno's personal indulgence.

Whatever the results of Sukarno's later policies, it must never be forgotten that he is the man, more than anyone else, who welded the country together, led it through the trials of the revolution, beat the Communist rebels and the Dutch imperialists, and kept Indonesia an independent country.

Mohammed Hatta, a scholarly type of person, logical in his thinking, and with a strong appeal to intellectuals, was an excellent teammate for Sukarno, and together they were the most basic heroes of the independence movement. While Hatta was a university student in Holland, he helped organize an Indonesian independence society. After Sukarno was arrested by the Dutch, Hatta went back to the Indies in 1932 and took over direction of that part of the freedom movement that later proved to be its head and heart. Two years later he was himself arrested, and he was held for eight years, first at a jungle outpost in New Guinea and later on one of the islands in Maluku.

Hatta and Sukarno were so closely linked during the revolution and the early years of the Republic that the expression "Sukarno-Hatta" was used as if for a single person. It was natural for Hatta to have, at different times, the titles of Vice President and Prime Minister, and for him to have been the key factor in national policy at many tense moments. He resigned as Vice President in 1956, and in later years he criticized Sukarno publicly. But their joint status as heroes is recognized by their present titles as "Proclaimers of Independence," and a national monument has been erected to them jointly.

Mohammed Hatta,
first Vice-President
of the Republic

Sutan Sjahrir, another of the leaders arrested when the Dutch paratroopers dropped on Yogyakarta in 1948, was a long-time companion of Hatta in imprisonment and exile. He also had been a university student in Holland, and he returned home when Hatta did. His moving and fascinating letters to his Dutch wife, published in English translation in America under the title *Out of Exile,* show the depth of the intellectual and spiritual experience through which the two men passed. They seem to have read at that time nearly everything from the Bible to Marx and Freud.

At the last moment, just before the Japanese invasion, the Dutch realized that Indonesian patriots such as Hatta and Sjahrir might be helpful in the defense. They arranged to have an American plane pick up Hatta and Sjahrir and bring them to Java.

Sjahrir was Prime Minister three times, a key negotiator with

Sutan Sjahrir, a leader in the revolution and three times Prime Minister

the Dutch, and the most important of all Indonesians in telling their story to the world when he came to present the case of the new Republic to the United Nations in New York.

During the war Sjahrir chose the dangerous course of the secret underground. He had his own organization that he directed while traveling around Java or posing as a laborer on a relative's place. He was in touch with other groups, including the Communists. He had secret meetings with Hatta, so that both the collaborators and the resistance knew what the others were doing.

Haji Agus Salim was the grand old man of Indonesian independence. Although he was a devout Muslim, he was alert to every modern trend in world scholarship. He lectured at several American universities, and to many people in the world he was "Mr. Indonesia." He combined modernism and piety in his attitude toward

Haji Agus Salim, an intellectual leader in the freedom movement

Islam and helped protect the Islamic branch of the independence movement from being taken over by Communism. With his tiny frame and wizened merry face, he represented a spirit and integrity that are treasured by all Indonesians. He was several times Foreign Minister and a perfect representative of his country before the world.

While these men were being held by the Dutch, the revolution was bravely continued by others. An emergency government was set up in Sumatra, out of Dutch reach, and the fighting in Java was carried on heroically under General Sudirman who, though a dying man, kept on leading the troops, even after he had become so ill that he had to be carried from place to place.

American public opinion was strongly with the Republic from the start. But our State Department was concerned with the defense of Europe against both Russian military threats and possible Communist takeover of weak European governments. Our government did not want to do anything in the Indies that would weaken Holland at home. But the Indonesians and their friends in the United States said that the many thousands of troops and hundreds of millions of dollars that Holland was using in trying to reconquer the Indies might better be used in Europe. They pointed out that the money Holland spent on military actions in the Indies was about equal to the total it was getting from America under the Marshall Plan.

As the facts became better known in America there were public demands, including some in the U.S. Senate, that we give the Dutch no more help at home until they had stopped fighting the Indonesians or at least had pulled back to the agreed truce line.

Meanwhile, Asian countries that had never before taken an important part in world affairs made clear their support for Indonesia. And the Soviet Union, always glad to get into the act as a friend of Asian peoples, gave its strong support also.

Finally, as a result of the many pressures, the Republican leaders were released and returned to Yogyakarta, and an Indo-Dutch conference was held at The Hague. There, on November 2, 1949, an agreement was signed recognizing the Republic of Indonesia as the sovereign power in all the former Dutch East Indies except New Guinea, which was left for later discussion. The two countries were to be in an Indo-Dutch Union under the symbolic leadership of the Dutch crown in somewhat the same way that free and sovereign Australia and Canada are members of the British Commonwealth. Some years later even this tie was cut, and Indonesia stood alone as one of the entirely free nations of the world.

On December 27, 1949, sovereignty was turned over to the Indonesians in Batavia, which was immediately rechristened and known after that as Jakarta.

The man acting for the Republic on this occasion was the Sultan of Yogyakarta, whose royal name is Hamengku Buwono IX.

Hamengku Buwono IX,
Sultan of Yogyakarta

His loyal public service enabled him to become a national hero in spite of republican prejudice against royalty. While certain other members of the royalty were scheming with the Dutch to betray the revolution, as a means of getting back their former thrones, the Sultan of Yogyakarta boldly threw in his lot with the Republic.

During the Dutch military action the sultan was a colonel in Indonesia's national army, and later he served as Minister of Defense in one cabinet and Deputy Prime Minister in two others. He took a leading role in the new government following the coup in 1965, and became Vice President when General Suharto was elected President by the People's Consultative Assembly.

During the fight for independence, ending in 1949, the Indonesians felt as the Americans did during the winter of 1777–78 in Valley Forge. They thought there could be no more difficult time for the Republic. But for both countries, the winning of independence was only the first step in a never-ending struggle to keep the freedoms that had been won and to make the government serve the welfare of all the people.

Personal selfishness as well as ethnic, religious, regional, and political differences harmed national unity and prevented the proper working of the democracy.

The religion of Islam helped to hold the country together. And modern Islamic ideas, many of them having come to Indonesia from Arab intellectual leaders in the 1920s, helped the movement for social justice. In the pre-independence debate among Indonesians about the form their country should have, one of the hottest issues was whether Indonesia should be an Islamic state, with religious law and influence controlling civil life, or a secular state with freedom of religion. The decision was for a secular state.

There had always been extremist Muslim groups, however, and one of them was especially active after independence. That was the organization known as Dar ul-Islam. It used terrorism and violence instead of democratic methods, and it seemed bent on changing the

Republic into a completely religious state. The Dar ul-Islam refused to obey civil authority, and it brought cruel vengeance to families, or even whole villages, that defied it. They ruled the countryside in the areas where they were strong, and some of their guerrilla bands held out for years in Sumatra, Kalimantan, Sulawesi, and the mountains of West Java.

But the worst continuing threat to Indonesian unity and independence came from the Communists. They were in decline for a while after Sukarno and his followers put down the rebellion in 1948. And Communist Party leaders in Moscow confused their Indonesian supporters by constant changes in the "party line." Communist strength began to return gradually, however, and in the decade from 1955 to 1965 there was an enormous gain in Party membership. There were plenty of flaws in the operation of the Indonesian government, and many people thought that alliance with the Communists was the simplest way of showing they did not like the way things were going.

Although Sukarno had opposed the Communists earlier, later on he encouraged them by his policy of "neutralism" and his effort at walking a tightrope both at home and abroad. Like many other Asian leaders, he wanted to keep out of the cold war between the U.S.A. and the U.S.S.R., yet at the same time he tried to keep Communist support for his policies at home and to continue receiving massive American economic and technical help. To Sukarno's critics the policy seemed to be not so much "neutral" as "playing both ends against the middle."

One of Sukarno's achievements in the international field was the organization and sponsorship of the Asian-African Conference in Bandung in April 1955. At that time the city of Bandung became the center of world attention. For a time Bandung swept both Moscow and Washington off the front pages of newspapers, and reporters from every nation on earth were in this delightful Indonesian city that most of them had never heard of a few months before.

Bandung has been for a long time the center of cultural life of the Sundanese people, and Bandung puppet shows are famous. But these were not the reasons for the worldwide interest.

The occasion was the Asian-African Conference called by Sukarno, the first meeting ever held of representatives of nearly all the peoples of Asia and Africa. The Bandung Conference was attended by Nehru of India, Nasser of Egypt, Chou En-lai of Communist China, Ho Chi Minh of Vietnam, and leaders of many other countries of the two continents.

Few actions of importance were taken at Bandung, but the conference was nevertheless one of the great dividing points of history. Before that time the peoples of the two continents, even those who had won full independence, continued to think of themselves as to some extent wards of Europe. At Bandung they suddenly realized their independent power.

But they were also struck, some apparently for the first time, with an awesome sense of their world responsibilities. They seemed in some ways like a student council that has been agitating for years for certain rights and then, having won them, is suddenly faced with the obligations that they had not realized would be handed to them along with the powers. Or one might think of a young American finally getting a driver's license and all at once realizing the responsibility placed on him when at last he finds himself alone behind a wheel.

Many world problems used to be handled by the older countries, often by deliberately excluding the new nations from participation. But now the developing countries recognized these were their problems also. Nothing was settled at Bandung, but that is the place where the Asian and African independence movements came of age.

The discussion of imperialism—the rule of colonies by other countries—was especially lively at Bandung. Many of the leaders present were former if not present revolutionists. They were accustomed to striking out at Britain, Holland, and other colonial powers as oppressors of subject peoples. They were so much in the habit that they went right on talking that way at Bandung, even though many of the physical battles against European imperialists had already been won. The problems of economic and intellectual imperialism would take longer to solve.

But some of the others pointed out that the end of one battle was near, while the Communist imperialism was an active and rising danger to Asian and African freedom. The conference ended by condemning imperialism of all sorts.

Sukarno's opening address was of special interest to Americans. He happened to be speaking on an anniversary of the ride of Paul Revere, and American reporters were startled to hear this mentioned by the leader of a new nation on the opposite side of the world. He called our American Revolution "the first successful anti-colonial war in history," and quoted from Longfellow:

> *"A cry of defiance and not of fear,*
> *A voice in the darkness, a knock at the door,*
> *And a word that shall echo forevermore!"*

"Yes," he continued, "it shall echo forevermore. . . . But remember, that battle which began one hundred eighty years ago is not completely won, and it will not have been completely won until we can survey this our world and say that colonialism is dead." And he mentioned "colonialism in modern dress" as being economic control or intellectual control by powerful groups within a country.

After the Bandung Conference, the Communists greatly increased their following. A more or less neutral foreign policy was approved by the majority of Indonesians, even by many who were among the strongest anti-Communists in their domestic situation. They wanted Indonesia to be loyal to itself rather than to any foreign power, whether the U.S., the Soviet Union, or China. So a policy of nonalignment was widely accepted in the country. But some of the domestic policies that Sukarno adopted with Communist support or under Communist pressure led to deep trouble. We shall look at these issues later.

In money matters, Indonesia was in constant trouble from 1942 onward. During the Japanese occupation the invaders were naturally interested in getting raw materials for their own use, rather than in building up the Indonesian economy. Then, during the fight for independence, the Indonesians felt they had to use a "scorched earth" policy against the Dutch in parts of Java and Sumatra. The Dutch blockade of Republican territory was of course harmful in itself. Production of both food and the sources of foreign income (oil, rubber, and so forth) naturally went down.

Then came the difficult period of trying to get the new Republic started, followed by one in which poorly trained or completely untrained Indonesians tried to take the place of Dutch technical specialists and managers who withdrew or had been expelled.

Indonesia might have recovered from those troubles if something still worse had not developed: internal corruption. On top of everything else came public realization that bribery, favoritism, and dishonesty of other kinds (from which the Indonesians thought they were freeing themselves when they took affairs into their own hands) were to be found in almost all branches of their national government. There was an unholy alliance between crooks and supposedly respectable public officials. The common citizens, and especially the students and other young people, felt more and more disillusioned. And the Communists were able to cite more and more examples of corruption and deference to special interests at the expense of the common good. Their propaganda efforts thus received increasing support from current events.

Because the central government was in Java, and the most active black marketers and corruptionists operated in the capital city of Jakarta, people in some of the Outer Islands, especially Sumatra, began to express anti-Java ideas with more and more violence. The Outer Islands thought that people in Java were seizing for personal gain the foreign-exchange income that was being produced by the labor and natural resources of the other islands. These contemporary economic differences gave fuel to the traditional cultural and ethnic differences and suspicions.

Finally, in 1958, full-dress rebellions were launched in Sumatra and Sulawesi. The leaders included men who had held important positions in the Republic: a governor of the Bank of Indonesia, a dean of the University, and a leader of one of the chief political parties. Furthermore, the rebels had support from the American CIA, reportedly in the hope of upsetting Sukarno, who appeared to be playing the Communist game. It looked once more as if Indonesia would fall apart.

But as so often in the past, Indonesia had surprises for the world. The government, and especially the army, moved with speed and efficiency. Even though some of the army units joined the rebels, the uprising was put down quickly. The leaders took to the hills or fled to Singapore and Hong Kong. The authority of the central government was confirmed once again.

Even more important for the future, the army's reputation gained a new polish. It was clear that the army was one of the three great forces in Indonesian political life, the two others being President Sukarno and the Communist Party.

The Sumatra-Sulawesi rebellions were not the only dramatic crises in which the army played a key role. Under a vigorous and attractive chief of staff, General Nasution, a pious Muslim, the army served as a kind of balance wheel in Indonesian politics. That tradition continued even after Sukarno had Nasution "kicked upstairs" to become Minister of Defense.

Meanwhile, the Communist Party under its skillful leader, Aidit, grew and grew in the 1950s and early 1960s. The Chinese replaced the Russians as its strongest influence from outside, but help continued to come from both countries. Within Indonesia itself the Communist Party was tightly organized, and it became the largest political party in the country and the third largest Communist Party in the world.

One of the defenses that has been made for Sukarno's policy of not permitting normal elections was that the Communists would have come to power if elections had been held. They were a minority in the total population, but no other party had so much voting strength or so much political power.

For a long time Sukarno was able to play off the army and the Communists against each other, while he himself held the balance of power. Most people, even many of Sukarno's harshest critics, agree that in this way he kept Indonesia non-Communist for more than a decade.

But in any event the time came in the early 1960s when Sukarno seemed to be siding more and more with the Communists, and to be letting them into the government. At the same time Sukarno himself acted with less common sense than before and against his country's interest. Besides personal indiscretions that angered many citizens, especially women (he was a polygamist at a time when great strides were being made toward monogamy), he annoyed the United States Government, which had been the chief source of economic help. He even took his country out of the United Nations and other international organizations that had given Indonesia indispensable help. Also, Sukarno led Indonesia into a kind of war (called *"confrontasi"*) with the neighboring country of Malaysia, to prevent a union of Malaysia with the Borneo territories of Sabah and Sarawak.

With all these things happening, the cumulative effect of frightful inflation, suspension of elections, use of dictatorial powers, and dismissal of Parliament, it looked in the summer of 1965 as if the country was ready to blow up.

But when Communists tried a coup, on September 30, 1965, the results were far different from what anyone had expected. The plot started with the brutal assassination of several army generals, including some who were held in special respect. The purpose was to get control of the army as well as of the civil government. But alertness on the part of loyal officers, and some error in the timing of an intended Communist uprising, prevented the plan from succeeding. For some hours the outcome was uncertain, but the non-Communist forces won out under General Suharto. He took control of the army and of the country.

The new government began with Sukarno as a symbolic leader, but his power as dictator was ended. His apparent awareness of the secret movement that had been underway gradually became known and lost him much of his one-time support.

In the meantime, however, the country in general went through one of the most frightful periods of its history. There were terrible mass executions of alleged Communists, many thousands of

General Nasution, who was chief of staff and Minister of Defense and for some years a balance wheel in Indonesian politics

whom were slaughtered without trials. The provocation for this bloody revenge was great, but the friends of Indonesia nevertheless deeply regretted this dark chapter in the national history.

General Suharto and his colleagues in the new government started the huge task of rebuilding the economy, of ending the war with Malaysia, of leading the country back into the society of nations, and of starting Indonesia moving once more toward the goals sought since independence.

Indonesia's economy was in desperate condition when Suharto took control. Much of the productive capacity was in disrepair through neglect and lack of spare parts. Furthermore, too much business energy had been drawn off over the previous ten years into pursuit of easy money through black-marketing and corruption instead of increasing production. The money value of the rupiah had gone down to a thousandth of its former worth. It was as if, in the

Adam Malik,
Vice-President,
Foreign Minister, and
one of the founders of
ASEAN

United States, a movie ticket that had once cost $3 should now cost $3,000. As this inflation went on there was great hardship for the common people, especially those in cities who had to buy their food instead of producing it on the land.

The new government of Suharto, though facing almost impossible problems, started out courageously with the help of some of the ablest leaders whose talents had been unused, or poorly used, during the recent years. The Sultan of Yogyakarta, the "royal democrat" whom we met earlier, was one of these. Another was Adam Malik, a revolutionary hero who became Foreign Minister and Vice-President, made frequent trips to the United States, and was widely admired in both socialist and capitalist countries. In 1971 he was elected President of the General Assembly of the United Nations. Dr. Sumitro, the country's top economist, was taken into the Suharto government as Minister of Trade, even though he played a leading part in the 1958 rebellion.

The new government was able to enlist from the university and elsewhere many of the "technocrats" and intellectual leaders who had served the country earlier but in recent years had been in disfavor with Sukarno or had been blocked off by the Communists. An example was Soedjatmoko, a distinguished publisher, journalist, and political leader who was recognized as perhaps the outstanding intellectual in the country. He had been in the first mission to negotiate Indonesia's entry into the UN, but through the years lost his influence with the government, had his newspaper suppressed, and in the first half of the 1960s was unable to serve his country at all. The new government, however, sent him first to the UN as Deputy Ambassador, and then to Washington as Ambassador to the U.S. Later he served as a consultant to the planning agency at home and then became rector of the United Nations University in Tokyo.

Friendly official relations were resumed by the new Suharto Government not only with the United States and European countries but notably with the neighbors: Singapore, Malaysia, Thailand, and the Philippines. Indonesia joined those four in forming the regional group called ASEAN (Association of Southeast Asian Nations), which has become one of the most effective regional groups anywhere.

Indonesian young people, especially university students, played a major part in the country's new political life. They had helped force the Declaration of Independence, and also helped bring about the defeat of the Communists and the downfall of the Sukarno government. By demonstrations and in other ways they kept pressing the government to get rid not only of the evils that had come in under Sukarno but also of his own power and influence. Some people at the time expected that there might be civil war because Sukarno still had a popular emotional following in parts of the country. So the new Suharto government moved cautiously. Little by little, how-

Soedjatmoko, Ambassador to the United States and later rector of the United Nations University in Tokyo

ever, they whittled away Sukarno's authority, and finally even his ceremonial function.

By 1967 Sukarno had withdrawn from the presidency, and was permitted to retire to his palace at Bogor. Passersby could see the beautiful gazelles still grazing on his front lawn, but little else remained of his past grandeur. Although bitterness continued against him for the many mistakes and misdeeds of his later years, his place in history is secure. At the time of his death in 1970 he was still honored as the founding father of the Republic, and enormous crowds of Indonesians followed the funeral procession to his burial place in East Java. In the years following his death, there were continuing evidences of his positive influence on the Indonesian people.

In 1971, in the first public test of President Suharto's power after the new government (officially called "The New Order") came in, the government won a strong vote of confidence. An association of organizations formed to support the government was called "Golkar" and came to be regarded as "the government party." Some of the old parties were forbidden to participate, but Sukarno's party, the PNI, and the conservative Muslim party, the NU, were allowed to contest for seats, and they were roundly defeated. The election was orderly, and the government's clear victory showed that a new era had begun.

In a later chapter we will say a bit more about the new era in Indonesia's history. But let us first take a closer look at the Indonesian people themselves and the way they live.

9

The Indonesian People

Indonesians are good-looking people. Most of them have well-formed features, perfectly turned limbs, and sturdy, graceful bodies. Skins are brown, varying in darkness from area to area. In the capital city of Jakarta, where there are people from all sections of the country, you see almost every shade. Many Indonesians have a facial appearance that foreigners often speak of, carelessly and inaccurately, as "Chinese." There are Chinese in the country, but they have tended to keep racially and culturally apart. The "oriental" appearance of the true Indonesians traces back, rather, to the old Mongoloid elements in the Malay people who invaded the whole area. Because of the common racial heritage among Southeast Asians, one is often unable to guess whether a given person is from Malaysia, Indonesia, or the Philippines.

Not only are the people good-looking, but they have a natural grace that is shown by laborers at heavy tasks as well as by delicate dancing maidens. And they have courtesy, poise, and, most of the time, incredible patience.

The Indonesians have continued about their daily work without violence during many incidents in the last dozen years that would have caused repeated explosions in many other countries. There have been occasional outbursts of popular violence, the mass murders in 1965 being the most tragic and most conspicuous. And students organized mass protests periodically through the 1960s and 1970s. Those demonstrations related to issues such as corruption, the imbalance between social and economic development, and limitations on personal freedom. But for much of Indonesia's modern history, persistence and *musyawarah*—the custom of postponing action until consensus is reached—served as a substitute for rioting.

The position of Indonesian women may have something to do with this, or may merely reflect it. Women have a higher, more useful, and more important place in Indonesia than in most countries of Asia, and certainly more than in any other Muslim country. The high status of women is not confined to educated classes in cities. Women in rural areas traditionally have been important in their families and villages. Royal ladies, on the other hand, tended to lead closed and almost useless lives. Therefore it is especially noteworthy that a royal princess could be a pioneer of women's freedom.

In the early twentieth century there were a number of woman activists who campaigned for better educational opportunity for women. The most famous was a Javanese princess named Kartini, who died in 1904 at the age of twenty-five. Even in that short life she started a revolution. She was one of the most charming and spiritually minded of all cultural heroines. She wanted, for herself and other Indonesian women, the right to play an active part in the world's work, freed from the restrictions of traditional Javanese customs. She was practical in what she did, but one of the most typical sentences from Kartini is: "I want to make myself worthy of the highest title, and that is a Child of God."

With the devoted help of Dutch friends, she acquired a good education in Indonesia. Then she started a school for girls, and later started another one in her new home when she married a Javanese prince.

Kartini's fame came with publication in Dutch in 1911 of letters she had sent to Dutch friends; this book became the basis of the women's movement in Indonesia. It appeared in English in an American edition in 1920 under the title *Letters of a Javanese Princess* and has been republished repeatedly. A girls' school was started in Kartini's memory in 1912, and her birthday, April 21, is observed each year as Kartini Day throughout the country. As an Indonesian woman journalist wrote in 1960, "Through her, Indonesian women saw the light."

The first building to be erected as a school for girls was the project of another princess, Dewi Sartika, a West Java pioneer in urging freedom and education for women. In Aceh one of the heroic figures was a woman, Cut Nyak Din, who was a crusader against the Dutch. And mention must also be made of another Indonesian woman, Rahmah El Yunusiyyah, a pioneer in education in the Minangkabau area.

The distinguished figures of the past have been followed in the

Maria Ulfah Santoso, first woman cabinet minister

recent period also. As part of Sukarno's remarkable achievement in bringing together all kinds of Indonesians—from every island and every way of life, the peasant alongside the sultan—he brought women prominently into public life. Women played a full part, often a courageous one, in the freedom movement. And after independence, women became more and more important in the life of the Republic.

Maria Ulfah Santoso was Minister of Social Affairs in an early cabinet, and thus probably the first woman cabinet officer in any Muslim country. Later she was executive assistant to a succession of prime ministers from different political parties and often the real key to the functioning of the Indonesian government. Artati Marzuki-Sudirjo was Minister of Basic Education and later was secretary-general of the Foreign Office. Rusiah Sarjono was Minister of Social Affairs, while Lasiah Sutanto was Associate Minister for the Role of Women in Development. Sri Widoyati S.H. was one of the earliest woman members of any Supreme Court in the world. In Hindu Bali one of the outstanding figures has been Mrs. Gedong Oka, a university professor who served in the national Parliament and led a unique development project based on Gandhian philosophy.

In all government departments there are offices directed by women, and men do not seem to have reservations about working with them or under their direction. But useful work by women is not limited to government jobs. In many other fields as well, women have proved to be Indonesia's "secret national resource." Even in business one finds the same thing. A study of batik, the major industry of the city of Bandung, as far back as 1957 showed that half of all the firms were run by husband and wife jointly and a quarter of them by women alone.

Two remarkable women in the private voluntary sector have been Dr. Yetty Rizali Noor and Johanna S. Nasution. Dr. Noor had been a guerrilla fighter in her youth and became internationally famous in the women's movement. She was a dentist by profession

Dr. Yetty Rizali Noor, onetime guerrilla fighter, later social reformer and worker for women's rights

Johanna S. Nasution, leader of the National Council of Social Welfare

and dean of a dental school, but was best known as a campaigner through her organization, Perwari, and in other ways for reform of the marriage code and for other social and political causes. Mrs. Nasution, wife of General Nasution, of whom we have spoken, performed such outstanding public service as head of the National Council of Social Welfare that she was given a Magsaysay Award, a Philippine honor that is called "the Asian Nobel Prize."

The condition of religion, as well as the position of women, reflects the tolerant spirit. Nine-tenths of the people are Muslim. The Hindu and Christian minorities are in general well treated. As a matter of fact, because the Christian tribes had better education from missionaries than the Dutch Government was giving to the people generally, there is a relatively high percentage of educated Christians. These people, and especially the Bataks from Sumatra, hold a higher proportion of important government jobs than we might expect from their tiny percentage in the total population.

Indonesian Muslims are distinct from the rest of Islam in various ways. Foreigners—even including some visiting Muslims from other countries—are sometimes fooled into thinking that "Indonesians don't take religion very seriously." That is a wrong idea, based on surface signs. These include the fact that Indonesian women do not wear veils; that most of the mosques, the places of worship, are not impressive compared with those in other Muslim countries; that the Minangkabau people still have "matrilineal" families, that is, tracing the line through the mother instead of the father; that everywhere Muslim law is mixed with customary local law; and that not many Indonesians have more than one wife, even though Muslim law theoretically permits four. But Indonesian Muslims are for the most part loyal and devout, and many thousands of them make the holy pilgrimage to Mecca each year. Islam is intensely important not only in Indonesians' personal lives, in their feeling of direct relationship with God, but also in public affairs.

Islam, like Christianity, is a daughter of Judaism. These three

faiths are "monotheistic," that is, believing in one God. They have
so much in common that an American finds it easy to understand
many of the main ideas of Islam. The word "Islam" means submission (to the will of God), and a "Muslim" is one who submits. Jesus
is deeply revered, and many of what might be called Christian
virtues are also Islamic virtues.

Just as the teachings of Jesus have, at different times in our own
history, been a force for social reform, Islamic ideals have sometimes
helped lead the way to change in Indonesia. Muslim parties have
figured largely in the political life of the Republic, as well as in the
fight for independence, the movement for social justice, and the
attack on spiritual emptiness, whether of Communism or of Western materialism. One of the great successes of Sukarno and the other
leaders was to combine the religious and nonreligious groups into
one powerful national movement strong enough to beat the Dutch
and keep the Communists from taking control. But after independence had been won and the Dutch troops had departed, it became
difficult to hold the groups together. Just as the Communists had
tried to "run away with the revolution" for their purposes, some
religious groups tried to seize control for their own reasons.

It must be understood, however, that the stated aims of both
Muslim and Communist groups—so different from each other but
sometimes so alike in method—have had wide support from Indonesians in general. The ideal state described by the Prophet Mohammed in seventh-century Arabia has a great appeal for many
twentieth-century Indonesian Muslims. And the ideals of social and
economic justice that the Communists said they were following are
naturally attractive to people exploited through long centuries by
their own princes as well as by foreign invaders.

Without wide education and knowledge of what has happened
under Communism in other countries, the simple Indonesian peasant or the city worker without property had a hard time believing
the warnings that non-Communists gave him. Only when Commu-

nists gained some measure of control and then failed to bring any improvement in the life of the individual citizen did widespread disenchantment set in.

Muslim groups have been the Communists' chief opponents. In the past the Masyumi was the largest Muslim political party; until it was ordered to disband in 1960, it was regarded as the strongest anti-Communist force. The Muslim spirit of the army is believed by some to be the reason for its generally non-Communist position. Islam is important in every phase of Indonesian life—not just on Friday (their holy day), but all the time.

But we have learned by now that nothing in Indonesia ever turns out to be just what we might have expected. The country's incredible ability to absorb and adapt and modify everything it gets from abroad applies in the field of religion as well as everywhere else. Beneath Islam are those layers of Hinduism and Buddhism and animism from still earlier eras. Even after all the centuries that have now passed since the Koran was brought to the Indies, old beliefs keep cropping up and old folk customs are intertwined with Islamic ritual.

Just for example, in spite of the Islamic rule against idols, in Indonesia some Muslims among village people, without any feeling that they are doing anything wrong, bring offerings to the great Hindu statue of Loro Jonggan ("Slender Maiden") in Central Java. The same sort of thing goes on in other parts of the country, with offerings to other statues, as well as to stones, graves, and trees.

The folklore of the peasants and the stories relating to their many festivals and ceremonies are filled with the special local brand of Hinduism, even in sections that have been completely Muslim for centuries.

There are even Javanese-Hindu legends that are used to point out Islamic morals, and that remain the basis for Javanese high culture, arts, drama, and dance. In the dramas, and especially in the puppet shows, the stories are of Hindu origin.

But because Indonesian culture is so complex, even Hinduism does not tell the whole story. Lying beneath everything else is the ancient animism, or belief in spirits, and ancestor worship going back to times even before the Hindus came.

Folkways whose origins are lost in the mists of centuries are still active forces in the life of Indonesia. The word that scholars use for the putting together of ideas from varied sources is "syncretism." For us it is enough to say that the Indonesians are absolute masters at taking a little here and a little there, molding them together, adding a touch of something left over from a few centuries earlier, and ending up with something uniquely Indonesian.

The same sort of drawing from many sources has occurred in many other fields besides religion. Many of the ideas have come from widely divergent traditions within Indonesia and from around the world. Economic ideas come from the old forms of village life, but there are also bits from the Dutch Culture System as well as typical capitalism of the Western world. Ideas of social reform have come from nineteenth-century social democracy and twentieth-century thoughts about the welfare state as well as from Indonesia's own traditions. Business is often based on methods from Europe, America, India, and China. Political thoughts have been taken from Jefferson, Marx, Roosevelt, Gandhi, Sun Yat-sen, Kemal Ataturk, and Mao Tse-tung. Manners and social customs are based on teachings from a wide variety of sources, from the legends of King Airlangga to the lively present-day instruction of movie stars.

One final characteristic of the Indonesian people should be mentioned before we turn to the subject of how they live. It is a nation of predominantly young people. More than 60 percent of the population is under the age of twenty-five—a fact of great economic and social significance.

10

How They Live

It is hard to describe directly what is going on in a people's minds and hearts, but sometimes we can get useful hints from outward signs. Let us take a look at houses, clothes, food, and the customs in Indonesia.

More than 80 percent of all Indonesians live in rural areas, and even those who have moved to the cities have carried many village customs with them. For instance, there is some similarity among most Indonesian houses, whether the design is old or new and whether the people live there in a life-style that is primitive or very modern. Side walls are not very important; what really matters is the roof. That is natural in a country where the weather is always warm, but where, in most sections, heavy rain can always be expected.

As a matter of fact, some houses, and even many public buildings, have virtually no side walls at all, but only screens of bamboo or palm matting that can be put in place for shading or for protection against a driving rain. Some houses do have heavy walls, which may be made of planks in some rural areas or masonry in Dutch-type houses in the cities, but even those usually have big doors and windows, to give an open effect. Decorated porches are used as living space and become important features of many buildings.

Variation of rooflines is one of the most distinctive signs of cultural differences. The roofs are made of nearly everything you

might think of—slabs of wood used like shingles, thatched palm
fiber, and lots of tile, usually red or salmon-colored. In some cities
red tiles are almost standard, but you also see them in country areas,
even though everything else about the house is flimsy.

Much of the "personality" and special character of the houses
come from those wonderful roofs. Among the most picturesque are
the thatched roofs of the Minangkabau people in Sumatra. Their
houses with richly decorated sides are regular museum pieces, especially if seen as a backdrop for colorful groups of people in local
costumes. But the crowning glory of these fascinating buildings is
the series of delightful upward-swooping roof-points. The small rice
barns, always near the houses, are miniatures in the same charming
style. There are few forms of home architecture in the world more
naturally pleasing to the eye than the Minangkabau houses.

In Madura there are splendid "buffalo horns" at the ends of the
ridgepole; the Batak and Dayak people have their own special forms
of roof; and in Jakarta the red tiles above white walls lost in greenery
make Americans think of Florida or southern California.

Wood carving, often gaily painted, has been one of the traditional arts in Indonesia for centuries, and there is some kind of
carving in almost all the different varieties of houses. Carving is seen
on pillars, rooftops, sidewalls, or porch ceilings. In some of the
communities, especially in Kalimantan, there are carved wooden
figures at the entrance to the living space to scare off demons.
Carvings of Hindu figures or symbols are found in all Balinese
villages.

In many areas the majority of the houses are raised on stilts a
few feet above the ground, and the entrance may be a short ladder
or kind of gangplank. The raised position keeps snakes and other
wild things from running in and out, it lifts the building out of the
mud, allows better circulation of air, and, in low areas, protects from
flood water.

An oddity of Indonesian houses from our point of view is that

One of the remarkable Minangkabau houses

"apartment houses" are found in the country but there have been few in the cities. In traditional rural areas we still find various interesting multifamily living arrangements. In Bali a clan might have a compound with several separate buildings for living areas of different branches of the family, for kitchen activity, for fulfilling religious obligations, for informal socializing and eating. The Minangkabau houses that we have discussed traditionally gain a new wing each time a daughter is married. In Kalimantan the tribes have wonderfully complex longhouses, something like the former longhouses of Iroquois in New York State, but elevated eight or ten feet in the air.

In the cities, until the 1970s there were almost no apartment buildings. While the density of people and the number living in each dwelling tended to be much higher than Americans are accustomed to, most of the city dwellings were individual houses. More comfortable city housing is usually still for a single family, all built on one floor and having some pleasantly landscaped green area.

A striking quality of all Indonesian housing, wherever it is, is that it is suited to the "extended family" concept. This is reflected even in modern urban housing: There are usually a huge veranda to invite and accommodate guests and more space for bedrooms than for living rooms—to take care of the "extended" families of several generations of the immediate family as well as cousins of varying degree, nieces and nephews, and so on.

Warm weather naturally affects clothing as well as houses, and the garments are proper for the climate. Indonesian men, like their brothers everywhere, tend to leave the fancier forms of dress to the ladies, except on special occasions, such as the brilliant traditional ceremonies when *everybody* puts on gorgeous traditional dress. Then the scene is in full technicolor. But on normal days the men in cities who are government officials, businessmen, office workers, and so forth dress very much as Western men would in a hot climate.

In less formal jobs, where an American might wear slacks and a sport shirt in the summertime, the Indonesian may have a handsome shirt of batik, the special fabric we shall describe later, or a practical wraparound sarong. Indonesian office workers have become so attached to Western appearances that some people with perfect eyesight have been accused of wearing horn-rimmed spectacles with plain glass, just for looks, and of carrying briefcases with nothing in them but a noonday lunch!

City workers in lower positions may go bare above the waist or wear white or colored or khaki Western-style shirts with open neck and short sleeves. These shirts, by the way, are usually remarkably clean, even when worn by manual laborers, in spite of the fact that there may be few washing facilities except a canal. Below the waist they wear either white or khaki shorts or a sarong. And the sarong is found in almost all country districts as a normal garment for men as well as women.

Shoes are usually worn outdoors in urban areas, but the custom of going barefoot in the house is common, and is adopted by many Westerners in Indonesia. It is not only cool but also a contribution to household cleanliness—no street dirt comes into the house on one's shoes. Outside of the cities, many of the millions of people have never had their feet in shoes. Even those of high economic station enjoy barefoot relaxation in their handsome city houses or mountain cottages, and they also often wear sarongs at home, much as American men may wear slacks or shorts on weekends, even though dressing formally during the working week.

The one article of clothing for men that can be seen everywhere is the black velvet cap called a *peci*, which has become almost a symbol of national unity. You see it worn by anyone from the President of the Republic to the lowliest peasant.

Although there is not normally a great deal of color in men's dress, the ladies more than make up for it. A tube of cloth (a sarong), or a length to wrap around the lower half of the body, called a *kain*, is the base of most women's outfits. A blouse of some sort is worn as a top. In Java and some other areas the blouse is customarily long-sleeved, fastens in front, is tightly fitted, and extends either just below the waist or to midthigh. An additional piece of fabric is usually worn loose over the shoulder. On formal occasions this might be something like elegant brocade, but for everyday wear this *slendang* can be put to practical use as a sling for carrying a baby or a load of packages. Women office workers tend to wear conventional Western dress, but traditional costume is still the most common dress for festive occasions.

Women's hair is drawn into a tight bun and decorated with tiaras, pins, clasps, combs, etc., made of shell, silver, gold, painted wood, and other gay materials. Flowers in the hair are frequent additions to the charm of the headdress. As a matter of fact, the Indonesians like to use flowers, singly or in the form of leis, on all occasions. In the famous Madura bull races, the animals themselves are decked with garlands.

Cotton is the most widely used cloth. It may be a cheap mass-produced print or a luxurious handmade batik. There are sections of

Harvested rice carried on a balancing pole

the country, out of touch with the cities, where clothing is of *tapa*, a fibrous material made by soaking and beating the bark of certain trees. And there are still primitive areas left in which ideas of what the well-dressed man or woman will wear go back so many centuries that a loincloth of leaves is the principal garment.

Umbrellas and parasols are used more for protection from the sun than from the rain. An attractive do-it-yourself umbrella frequently seen along the roadway is a banana leaf, picked up on the spur of the moment and held over the head.

Transport is a special problem in this country of mountains, islands, jungles, and swamps. Not much railroad trackage is found outside Java. Inter-island boats are much more important. An extensive and increasingly dependable domestic air service provides at least one daily flight to and from every province.

The system of roads, though far from complete, has had priority attention from the government and has shown dramatic improvement. At the same time there has been a great increase in the number of trucks in the country.

But in spite of those developments, the human body is still the chief means of transport. Women, especially, carry enormous loads on their heads. This is supposed to be the reason for the fine straight posture, and also for the habit of holding the head still and turning only the eyes when looking up or down or to one side.

The most common of all roadside sights in Indonesia is a porter with heavy loads—fruit, rice, coconuts, or something else—at the two ends of a long "balancing pole" across his bare shoulders. To control the bouncing of the load with each step, the porter has a special humping gait to reduce the up-and-down motion of the pole. It looks like the heel-and-toe pace used in Olympic walking races.

For a long time there were few taxis in even the largest cities. Their place was filled by vehicles called *becaks* or bicycle-rickshaws— although technically that is not right because the becak has *three* wheels, so it might better be called a tricycle pedicab. This is the normal form of transport for common people in cities and small towns. At one time there were more than 100,000 of them in Jakarta. Nowadays their operation is forbidden on main highways and avenues and in busy sections of the city.

In some cities the taxi service is provided by a horse-drawn cart, similar to what the British call a dogcart, and therefore called a *dokar* in some parts of Indonesia. It is pulled by a sturdy relative of the small wild horse from Central Asia.

Of course the bicycle is one of the most important vehicles for personal transport for most Indonesians in villages and small towns, and especially among students in the cities. And, nowadays, even in remote rural areas the roads may be crowded with *bemos* (three-wheel taxis), *helicaks* (motorized becaks), *oplets* (small buslike vehicles originally made from worn-out Opel automobiles), and, most numerous of all, Japanese-made pickups and vans.

Besides horses, the most numerous domestic animals are water buffalo, cattle, chickens, goats, pigs, sheep, cats, and dogs. The enormous water buffalo, the carabao, is a descendant of the wild ox, and has horns often measuring six feet across. It is the "living tractor" of the rice fields. The chickens are almost all very small, which seems right, because the kind of hen that we call bantam came originally from Banten in western Java.

Because good Muslims do not eat pork, pigs are found most often in the Hindu and Christian areas.

Primitive tribes that depend on hunting for their meat use spears, bows and arrows, blowguns with poison darts, and various kinds of traps. Their game includes deer, pheasantlike birds, monkeys, and wild boar.

Outside of the hunting tribes, Indonesians on many of the

Becaks (bicycle-rickshaws) in Jakarta

islands are not great meat-eaters. Except in Hindu Bali there are no religious overtones in their vegetarianism, but meat is not plentiful and not regarded as essential in tropical climate. Indeed, an American who took a Labrador retriever to Indonesia found that, in spite of the dog's reputation as a carnivore, he got along very well on a diet of rice, spinach, and carrots!

Rice is the staff of life in much of the country. Picturesque terraces marching up the hillsides and the paddies on the plains are typical features of the landscape in Java, Bali, southern Sumatra, and southern Sulawesi. The term "paddy," which we use for a rice field, is used by the Indonesians for the rice itself. They spell it "padi," and refer to "a field of padi."

The "wet-rice culture" of the richest part of the country is marvelously productive, and gives two or three crops a year. Where the soil is less good or water not available, or where farmers have not come to the aid of nature in the same way, the "dry-rice" method is used.

Without irrigation there is a much poorer yield. The dry method is also called "burn and plant," and that is a good description. Farmers clear and burn an area of jungle, plant the crop over and over again until the land is worn out after a dozen years or so, and then move on to a new patch.

The wet-rice system is interesting in a number of ways besides the main question of food supply. For one thing, it was the wet-rice system that brought prosperity to certain areas, making possible a high state of culture and the civilized refinement of such arts as dance and music. It also helped develop engineering skills and scientific planning for the irrigation system of dams, ditches, bamboo aqueducts, and water elevators powered by the flowing water itself.

But the greatest effect of the irrigated method of growing rice is that it teaches fair play, tolerance, and cooperation. It is a kind of primary school for democracy. An individual peasant could not afford to build a whole irrigation system just for his one small plot.

But by teamwork, a group of neighbors can do it together. And having done it, they cannot help learning about joint management of their project. The spirit of "live and let live" is found wherever there is sharing of water for the rice fields.

Thieving birds will eat up an entire rice crop if they are allowed to, so much effort goes into driving them away. Little windmills that whir as they turn may be set up among the paddies, or a child may be posted to shout and clap his hands. But most interesting of all is a cooperative system that, like irrigation, teaches the idea of helping one another.

A platform on stilts is set up in the middle of a wide group of rice paddies, and overhead strings lead to bells or rattles in all the fields, some of them hundreds of feet away. One guardian of the crop can watch the whole area and, by pulling the proper string, make a noise in the field that is being invaded. Owners of the different fields take turns supplying a boy for the job.

In the eastern islands generally, and in parts of Kalimantan and elsewhere, sago takes the place of rice as the chief food. The sago palm has a spongy center rich in starch. The tree is cut down, this central pith is cooked, and we can say that people in the sago area quite literally live on trees! In some areas, corn is the staple food.

Even in the rice areas an important additional food is the cassava, the source of tapioca. It came originally from South America. Its rootstock has even more starch than a potato, and it is cooked according to many local methods, some of which produce a paste something like the famous *poi*, which our own Hawaiians make from taro root. In acreage planted, the cassava comes next after rice and corn. There are some nutritional faults in cassava, however, and in recent years the government has been discouraging too exclusive a dependence on cassava. One of the good things about cassava is that it grows fairly well in soil much too poor for rice.

Yams, soybeans, eggplant, and peanuts are among other important food crops. Peanuts figure in festive meals in a way that is new

Fishermen preparing to set out in their small boats

to us. Bits of meat are broiled on skewers, like shish kebab but tiny in size, and are coated with chopped peanuts.

For cultivation of all these crops, the work is done by hand labor and by simple plows pulled by buffalo or oxen. The handmade iron hoe called a *pacol* is the most usual hand tool. Tractors are used to a limited extent on some of the big plantations growing cash crops, but most of the fields are too small for tractors; foreign machinery is much too expensive and hand labor very cheap.

Coconuts are both a major food source and a cash crop for export. Most of the cooking oil used in Indonesia is pressed from the coconut meat.

Fish are abundant and becoming more so with development of both ocean fishing and the inland fish culture. Among the most unusual ways of life in the whole country is that of the "sea gypsies." These are fishing people who literally spend their lives in their small boats, not like dwellers in shore-tied houseboats so frequently seen elsewhere in Asia, but true seafarers who keep to the open ocean a great deal of the time, even during furious storms.

Of all the good things to eat that grow in Indonesia, nothing pleases the foreign visitor more than the plentiful fruit. Perhaps the most frequently seen is the papaya, which seems to grow with the speed of light. In seven or eight months it develops from a seed to a twelve-foot tree bearing fruit. Bananas are in dozens of varieties and sizes and flavors. Some of them are twice as big as any we can buy in this country. Pineapples are abundant.

More unusual fruit include the jackfruit, the mangosteen, the rambutan (looking like a sea anemone), the mango, and the durian. The last is an evil-smelling fruit, yet it has a wonderful flavor. An English traveler described the smell as "sweet drains" (British slang for a sweet-smelling sewer), but one American fancier wrote that the durian tastes like pineapple ice with crushed cashew nuts.

As in all of Asia, whatever affects the crops is a matter of life and death to the people. It is not surprising, therefore, that religious functions and folk festivals are connected with the planting season, the growing season, the harvest season, and the warding off at all times of evil spirits.

Such festivals are colorful affairs, and they take many different forms, but almost all involve music, dancing, drama, and the finest costumes the village can produce. There are ceremonies of many other sorts during the year also, marking every stage of human life from birth to death. Some of these are peculiar to small areas, others are quite similar on different islands. Some of the occasions, such as the Madura bull races, have become internationally famous in the same way that the snake dances of our Navaho Indians, at first a purely local custom, have become known around the world.

Wedding ceremonies illustrate the principle of "Unity in Diversity," for although they are quite different from each other in many ways, a foreigner can see similarities among the different Muslim areas, and even likenesses between those and the functions of the Hindus on Bali and the Christians in Maluku. The one common element in the varied cultures of all the islands is a love of music, drama, and the dance. We will examine that richest field of Indonesian art in the next chapter.

II

Music, Dance, Drama,

and the Arts

Music, dance, and theater—but theater of a very special sort—are among the oldest as well as the greatest glories of Indonesian culture. Most of us in the Western world have just begun to learn about them. They are so different from the forms we know that they seem very strange at first.

For some centuries Europeans who went to the Indies thought that the music they heard there was crazy, most of the dances boring, and the dramas of a kind that no one would understand. The all-night performances were so tiring that the weary foreigner usually just gave up.

But little by little, careful Dutch, German, English, and American students have unfolded to us the unsuspected wonders of these Indonesian arts. And thanks to traveling companies of dancers and their orchestras in our own country from time to time, we can sometimes see and hear for ourselves.

Our understanding has improved in recent years, mainly because Western students of this music are taking a new approach: they not only study it but also learn to play it. At UCLA, Professor Mantle Hood, one of the most devoted students of this music in America, trained groups to play and make recordings of both Javanese and Balinese music. Wesleyan University has been another of the centers of such study in this country, and Cornell University has added musical performance to its extensive program of Indonesian studies.

Actually, the very first report on these arts in the English language was favorable, even though little improvement in understanding was made for some centuries after that. When that old sea dog Sir Francis Drake visited the Indies in 1580, he had his ship's musicians entertain a local king. The compliment was returned when the king had *his* orchestra perform. Drake recorded that he had heard this king's "country-musick which, though it were of a very strange kind, yet the sound was pleasant and delightful."

If Drake had gone on to talk about the instruments making the pleasant sounds, we should probably find out that they were about like those in use today four centuries later. Although there is variation in the form and level of sophistication of the music in different parts of Indonesia, in some areas there has been little change in the classical instruments and the music they play. Today, through TV, public school programs, and a network of government-sponsored schools of performing arts, there has been a great growth in understanding and appreciation of Indonesian music and other performing arts. But each distinctive form retains its strong regional connections and is performed most often in its area of origin.

The dance, drama, and music cultivated by the ruling classes in Java and Bali became the most widely known of the performing arts in Indonesia and have been the most thoroughly studied by Westerners. But gradually we have been becoming familiar to at least some extent with those arts as practiced in other parts of Indonesia. And the Indonesians themselves, who did not use to know about dance and music forms away from their own provinces, now follow with interest the folk arts of the entire country.

The process of learning about the arts of other sections of the country has naturally gone furthest in the capital city of Jakarta. Not only are people from all areas living there, but there are three institutions making a special point of sponsoring presentations of arts and crafts from the entire country. These are the Taman Ismail Marzuki, the Taman Indonesia Indah, and the Taman Impian Jaya Ancol (familiarly called "Binaria"), which is a kind of Indonesian Disneyland.

The kind of Indonesian orchestra heard most frequently in Java and Bali is called a *gamelan*. It plays a big part not only in dances and dramas but also in the festivals and folk ceremonies constantly held throughout the islands.

Most of the instruments are beaten or struck, but their effect

Bride doing a ritual dance while awaiting the groom

A gamelan orchestra in Bali

is no more percussive than that of a piano, because they are so finely tuned and have such a sweet sound.

The basic instruments are drums, metal bars, and gongs. The drums are the lead instruments. The gamelan does not have a leader out front to direct it. Instead, the players listen to one another and match their speed to the speed of the drumming. The metal bars are arranged in sets and played like xylophones in high, middle, and low range. We have Indonesia to thank for the word *gong* and its meaning. The large gongs of the gamelan are shaped like the lids of large frying pans. They have a deep rich sound that goes on and on. Many people think that an Indonesian gong gives one of the world's most beautiful instrumental effects. The smaller gongs, shaped like pots, have a lighter, higher sound, and often are arranged in sets so that melodies can be played on them.

There is a bowed string instrument from Central Asia that came with the Muslims to the Javanese courts. Only the most experienced musicians play it, for it is the most difficult of all the instruments and gives the melodic voice that the others follow. And there is a woodwind, a flute of bamboo that is played vertically like a clarinet rather than crossways like our flute. This instrument improvises delicate decorations for the main gamelan melody during soft sections of the music.

In some sections of the country there are fascinating additions to the list of instruments, though these are often played in other combinations rather than in gamelan orchestras. These instruments are different from anything we have seen in the West, except for certain drums that look like tambourines without the jingles, other drums that look like congas but with two heads, and Jew's harps entirely of wood, frequently bamboo. The unusual instruments include drums made of hollowed logs or lengths of bamboo, hand cymbals not played together but against a cluster of similar cymbals tied upside down to a board on the ground, bamboo xylophones, and an instrument like our violin but with the sound of a viola, and metal-strung zithers built like small slanted tables.

In Sulawesi there is a marching flute-and-drum corps. Especially in Java and Sumatra, but to some extent in other sections also, there is wide use of a bamboo instrument called an *angklung*, that seems to have originated with the Sundanese. It is a kind of tuned rattle made of tapered lengths of bamboo loosely hung in a wooden frame and giving a sound like a xylophone. Each instrument has a fixed tone, and the player holding the angklung gives it a shake each time the music calls for that note. The angklung is very popular with youth groups, and is valued not only for its music but also for teaching teamwork. Incidentally, angklungs have been made tuned to Western scale as well as in Indonesian tuning.

All instruments, even including the sophisticated gamelan, are important in village life. Although the most famous gamelans came down from royal families, the importance of a gamelan to any Javanese community must be stressed. Even nowadays a gamelan is one of the first purchases by a community that is just beginning to prosper and has some common village fund. Communities of Javanese who have settled in the Outer Islands immediately start saving for their "village gamelan."

The intricate music played by the gamelan is not written down. It is passed from teacher to student through one generation after another. That was one of the things that troubled the early Europeans. Those rough-and-ready merchants and adventurers, even those from educated classes and with knowledge of music at home, were really perplexed about the absence of any written notes. And because they themselves were unable to hear anything that sounded like a melody in the strange scales, they decided it was just undisciplined sound and not really music at all.

Composing the music and arranging it for an orchestra may follow a method something like that of a modern combo's jam session in America. That is, the composer-arranger gives ideas on his own instrument, while the others follow his lead, but make inventions and new contributions of their own.

The gongs have special meaning in dividing the musical phrases. Gongs of different size and tone indicate the ends of large or small sections of the melodic line.

In the Christian sections of Sulawesi and Maluku, hymns and other Western music became known fairly early. And in various parts of the country there is now growing interest in our music, both classical and popular. The stirring national anthem, *Indonesia Raya*, is in a Western scale.

There are even cases in which a Western theme is combined with the Indonesian themes of a gamelan. Modern popular songs are written in Western scale, and are often heard on the radio. And the angklung we mentioned has been adapted to our scale. Groups of young people in Bandung and Jakarta can be heard lustily singing such tunes as "My Bonnie Lies Over the Ocean" and "Home on the Range" with angklung accompaniment.

The dancing with which gamelan music is connected is really a form of drama. There are folk dances, and the general population takes part in these. But the best known Javanese and Balinese dances and many of the others are performed by specially trained people for an audience. Usually they tell a story.

Each gesture has definite meaning for the onlookers. Westerners seeing Indonesian dancing for the first time appreciate the graceful movements, but are usually surprised to discover that legs and feet are the least important parts of the body for these beautiful movements. Often, in fact, the dancer may be seated or squatting

An episode from the "Ramayana" in a Javanese folk dance

down for much of the dance. The arms, fingers, head, eyes, and neck do most of the dancing.

Westerners find it almost impossible to copy the motions exactly, even after years of practice. For instance, the apparently simple gesture of forming a *perfect* circle with thumb and forefinger, and snapping it open and closed, is something nobody from the West has ever been able to do to the satisfaction of an Indonesian.

The best dancers begin their training as children, and in some areas, such as Bali, the girl dancers usually stop performing when they enter their teens. There is always a spirit of youth and freshness, as well as incredible grace and precision, in this age-old Indonesian art.

A wayang-orang (human puppet)

Nearly all the dances require special costumes, and these are often of great brilliance and richness. Elaborate masks are also worn for some of the performances, and there are often stage properties such as fans, flowers, parasols, lighted candles, saucers, and the wonderful ceremonial sword or dagger called a *kris*.

The plot or scenario of each dance is known to the audience. That does not spoil their enjoyment. On the contrary, they like to "know how the story is going to turn out." They anticipate each gesture, and they know the inner meaning of every movement.

As we would expect from other things we have learned about the country, some of the stories are from ancient folk legends, but many had their origin in the great books of India, though changed to the new conditions in Indonesia. Some, also, deal with current events, especially the fighting against the Dutch during the Revolution and against the Communists later on.

Americans do not take puppet shows very seriously. At least we would not think of a Punch-and-Judy as a natural way of presenting religious ideas or ethical teachings. But puppets seem to Indonesians to be one of the highest forms of dramatic art. And they are absolutely tireless in watching the shows that they love so much. A typical performance may begin at 9:00 P.M. and end at 6:00 A.M.

Javanese puppets are of different kinds, but all are called *wayang*. The word means shadow, and the most familiar sort uses silhouettes held up to a screen lighted from behind. But there are other kinds of puppets in three dimensions. One sort of full-scale drama with human actors is called *wayang-orang* because orang means man. The reference to shadows in all these forms of theater, even if they are not shadow plays, is explained by the Indonesians in a beautiful way. They say that a drama is a shadow of life, and that man is a puppet of God. There is a moving poetic prayer, "O Lord, make me a wayang in thy hand," that is close in spirit to the Book of Psalms.

The popularity of wayang gives the final proof—if any were

A dalang holds a wayang-kulit against the screen

needed by this time—of local influence on foreign ideas, even if they are as strong as the religion of Islam. As we have noted, representations of the human figure are supposed to be forbidden in Islam. Yet here are the pious Indonesian people giving their enthusiastic approval not merely to pictures but to figures in the round. The flat grotesque puppets, which are the most popular in Java, may have been a Muslim substitute for the more lifelike figures used before the coming of Islam. This possibility is suggested by the fact that in Hindu Bali the earlier type continued without a break.

The most popular form of shadow play is called *wayang-kulit.* The figures are flat cutouts made of buffalo hide, stiffened with a gluelike substance, and magnificently painted in gold and other colors. Each has a horn handle. They are works of art in themselves.

The wayang performances, found chiefly in Java and Bali, are all-night affairs, and there is a relaxed and informal mood in the audiences. People come and go at will, carry on casual conversation during slow passages, and often move around during the performance. They may sit first where one can see only the shadows on the screen, but then change to a place where they can see the puppets themselves.

For the screen, a white cloth is stretched on a bamboo frame with a light behind it. This can be an electric light in a city, but much more frequently it is a coconut-oil lamp. At the bottom of the screen, lying horizontally, are two soft trunks of banana trees into which the puppet handles can be stuck. The gamelan orchestra, which is part of every wayang show, is also behind the screen.

Our American expression "as busy as a one-armed paper-hanger" is a fair way of describing the activity of the conductor of the wayang show. He is called the *dalang*. He must be, all at the same time, the speaker of the story, the handler of the puppets, the conductor of the orchestra, and the creator of special sound effects. He sits at the bottom of the screen, and holds up the flat puppets so their shadows are on the sheet. Because so many of the puppets represent noble or royal figures, they must never be disrespectfully placed below the dalang's head.

At one side of the dalang is the orchestra and at the other his chest of equipment, holding not only the collection of puppets but also noisemakers of bamboo and metal.

The stories, though impossibly long for an American viewer, and including bits of history and legend that are strange, use general themes that are not too unusual for American movie or TV viewers. Some of the characters are different—demons, etc.—and there are mystic swords and sacred figures not found in our movies. But the struggle is still between the good guys and the bad guys, or sometimes the effort of the boy to get the girl. Unlike Western drama, however, the conclusion most often indicates a continuing dynamic tension between good and evil, rather than a resolution with the triumph of the good.

A wayang-golek (three-dimensional puppet)

Even the plays with deep religious meaning, given on religious occasions, have a lively quality of exciting popular drama. The puppets have a strong hold on the public interest, whether shown in a permanent theater in a city such as Bandung or by a traveling dalang who goes into the farthest parts of the back country.

The flat puppets are of great artistry, but those in three dimensions, the *wayang-golek*, are even finer examples of carving, molding, and decorating. They have the same craftsmanship shown in other Indonesian arts that have come down through the ages.

We have already mentioned the skill of Indonesian wood carvers in connection with the houses, and every American visitor to Bali is likely to bring home one of the elongated carved figures for which the island is famous. So, too, with pottery and metalwork of many kinds. Silver filigree as delicate as a spiderweb is a specialty of some sections, and the glasses, pitchers, and bowls in solid tin are so tastefully designed that they are often used on fine tables in place of silver.

In an earlier time the highest level of art was reached in the design of arms and armor, especially the *kris*. This small sword or dagger was originally an actual weapon, but has now become a symbol. Even today there are art collectors who regard a perfect kris as one of the most beautiful objects to be seen in Indonesia. The workmanship of the metal blade is only the beginning. The handle and scabbard have the same splendor of design. The kris has sacred and magical importance, making it a necessary part of certain traditional ceremonies if they are to have ritualistic validity.

Even in the field of toys and casual playthings for children, Indonesian artistry is shown. Beautiful and entertaining toys are made from paper, bamboo, clay, wax, banana leaves and stems, coconut shells, palm leaves, and other simple materials. There is an endless variety of play hats, parasols, kites, wriggling "snakes," rattles, and other noisemakers. American children visiting in Indonesia have been known to abandon their own expensive mechanical toys and turn with joy to these attractive examples of Indonesian folk art.

But of all Indonesian handicrafts the best known both at home and abroad is the fabric dyed by the method called batik. Nowadays there is a great deal of mechanical or semimechanical printing of cloth, but the ancient method of making hand-batik is still used to some extent.

Melted beeswax is applied to the cloth from a little pitcher of a special shape. The wax is put on in lines according to the design that has been planned ahead of time. Then, when the waxed cloth is dipped in the dyeing vat, the color "takes" only on the unwaxed portions. After the first dyeing, the wax is scraped away, a new design is applied in wax, a new color of dye is used for the dipping, and so on until the full design is finished in all its colors. The job is so difficult that two months are frequently needed for good work, and

Hand operation in making batik

as many as six months may be given to batiking a sarong of special quality.

There is some use of the "tie-and-dye" method used by American home dyers, but it may be a more delicate operation than we normally see. The Indonesians sometimes tie tiny thread-ends in a careful pattern, rather than whole sections of the cloth.

We noted, when talking about houses, the great skill and sense of design in the painting of wood. As far as design is concerned, the making of batik is quite similar to that. But formal painting on canvas is an art that was slow in developing. This is rather surprising, because the Dutch came to Indonesia in considerable numbers during the Golden Age of Dutch painting, and are even said to have brought occasional Rembrandts and Vermeers with them. However, the painting of canvas was not important in the Indies, and there was such slight cultural contact with the Europeans that painting as an art form (as opposed to the decoration of objects and buildings) did not get its real start until quite modern times.

Indonesian sculpture, on the other hand, has had a background of many centuries, with Hindu and Buddhist as well as traditional animist influences. The international market for Balinese wood sculpture has been so active recently that there has been concern that the pressure for quick production may lower the standards of quality.

In fact many Indonesians as well as foreigners fear that imports of Western arts, or local copies using cheap mass-production methods, may tend to drive out local arts and crafts. They fear that the transistor may replace the gamelan, or that cheap cloth prints may end the handmade batik industry, or movies and TV finish the centuries-old art of the wayang.

There is indeed a danger that the marvelous creative spirit of Indonesian art may suffer from these modern trends. But the friends of Indonesia will hope that—as so many times in the past and in so many different ways—Indonesia may be able in this case also to take from the rest of the world without destroying the fine inner quality of its own artistic life.

12

Language and Education

Some hundreds of different languages are spoken in Indonesia. Many of them are quite unrelated to other tongues and are unintelligible to people living outside the area. The three major languages are spoken by enormous numbers: Javanese by 59 million, Sundanese by 28 million, Batak by 8 million. There are a half-dozen other languages spoken by 1 to 3 million each, and dozens and dozens of others whose use is confined to a small area.

Yet in spite of this mixture of tongues still used in family and village life in the different sections, the country has managed to gain general acceptance for one national language. That is called Bahasa Indonesia ("the Indonesian language"), and the story of its growth in the last fifty years is truly remarkable.

Usually languages grow slowly and change slowly. Even the daily users often fail to see what is happening to the language they speak. But the growth of the Indonesian language, and its spread over the entire country, resulted from conscious action by the leaders of the freedom movement and acceptance of their initiative by the public. Few cases can be found in history in which a deliberate decision about language has been so successful, and in which the new language has been so quickly adopted by so many people.

Most of the languages in Indonesia belong to the general family called Malayo-Polynesian, which is found not only in Southeast Asia but also through the Pacific Islands. Even the United States can claim a tiny corner of this vast linguistic empire, because the original language of one of our states, Hawaii, belongs to the same family.

Of the various branches of the language, the one called Malay, though not spoken by the largest number of people, was the accepted way for traders from different areas to talk with each other throughout Southeast Asia. Some knowledge of Malay thus spread quite widely, especially in port cities, throughout the Indies. Because of this contact with people from abroad, words from other languages crept into the Malay vocabulary. The resulting dialect was sometimes called "port Malay" or "bazaar Malay," that is, Malay used in the market.

During much of the centuries of Dutch rule there was little education of any kind for Indonesians. Then, under the Ethical Policy at the start of this century, schools were started for Indonesians, but using the Dutch language. The small percentage of people getting an education were almost entirely upper class. They studied Dutch books and wrote in Dutch; the few who went abroad at all for an education went to Dutch universities.

It is ironical, but not surprising, that much of the early protest against foreign rule was not in a local language but in Dutch.

But a great groundswell was coming to the surface among the people themselves. In 1924, for example, a sensation was caused when a cultural hero named Jayadiningrat gave a speech in Malay in the Dutch-sponsored People's Council, of which he was a member. Both the largest Muslim party and the Communist party used Malay, and in 1928 a landmark youth congress took the famous pledge "One people, one nation, one language." A lively group of young writers started a magazine called *Poejangga Baru* ("New Literary People") that helped make the use of Malay fashionable among patriotic intellectuals. Or rather, the language they were promoting was now becoming known as Indonesian.

Because Indonesian is not known in other countries, some

world language is needed for access to general knowledge and literature and to conduct foreign business. Before independence Dutch
was of course the language used for this purpose. But Dutch is itself
a minor language. So in part for that reason and in part because of
an emotional turning away from Indonesia's own colonial connections, English was made the official foreign language. An unexpected
push was given to the national language during the Japanese occupation. When Dutch (theretofore the method of communication
among educated people) was banned by the Japanese, there was an
extra incentive to learn Indonesian.

Besides Indonesian and a foreign language, however, Indonesians have their own local languages. To show how far this can go,
consider the friends of the author to whom the first edition of this
book was dedicated, the Hassan Shadilys. Mr. Shadily is from the
island of Madura. He talks his native Madurese with his mother,
Indonesian with business associates, Dutch and Indonesian with his
wife, who is a Minangkabau from Sumatra, Javanese with house
servants, and excellent English with his American friends. He also
has some French and German from school, some Japanese from
wartime, and some Arabic from the Holy Koran.

It seems unfair that people who take to languages so naturally
should themselves have one of the easiest. Any readers of this book
who have been studying French or Latin or German would be
overjoyed with Indonesian. It is a sheer delight for the beginning
student, as it is without conjugations, declensions, case-endings,
gender-endings, or subjunctives. There are no articles. Verbs and
adjectives do not have to agree with nouns.

Most of the time there is not even a difference between singular
and plural. When the Indonesians have to show a plural idea but no
number is mentioned, they repeat the noun. So "buku" means book
but "buku-buku" is books.

But there is another virtue in the language besides the lovely
simplicity of grammar and the easy pronunciation. There are many

words taken from other languages. Some of those are languages that most Americans do not know, especially Arabic and Sanskrit, the literary language of ancient India. But there are many words from Latin that are familiar to us through English, French, or Spanish. A large number are Germanic words that reached Indonesia through Dutch, but also have similar forms in English. Then there are the words that Indonesia took straight from English, either via British or Yankee traders in the old days or during the Raffles period of British rule, or, in most recent years, from the close contact with America.

We need no dictionary to tell us the meaning of words such as *universitas, presiden, Januari, Pebruari, tilpon, tilgram, eksekutif, kongres,* and *industri.* And then there are words that we might not guess on first sight but will never forget once we have learned them. Examples of those might be *es* for "ice," *Inggris* for "English," *saus* for "gravy," *kursus* for "course," *akuntan* for "accountant," *portret* for "photograph," *speda motor* for "motorcycle," and *pulpen* for "fountain pen." In modern science and technology most of the words come from the same international form, often based on Greek, from which we get our terms in English.

A final comfort of Indonesian for the beginning student is the fact that the language is written in the same roman letters used for English and other European languages. Lest we take that big fact for granted, we should remember that Indonesian is the only major Eastern language except Turkish that is written in the roman alphabet. Malay was formerly written in the beautiful but difficult Arabic script, reading from right to left.

An interesting thing has happened in relation to Malay, the mother tongue of Indonesian. Malay is the national language of the neighboring country, Malaysia. Because the Indonesian people outnumber the Malaysians about ten to one, we can say the daughter has grown much larger than the mother. And the new language is having a strong influence on the old one, just as American English has affected its parent, British English. In the case of the two forms of Malay, however, differences are bigger. The Indonesians used "tj" for the Malaysians' "ch" sound, for instance, so there were big differences in alphabetical order. Over a period of years there was talk about standardizing the spelling. In 1960 scholarly teams from the two countries drafted a plan for doing that. Political troubles delayed ratification for a long time, but the plan was finally put into effect. Now there is full uniformity in spelling.

At the earlier time, when the decision for a national language was made, Javanese might have been chosen because it was known to much the largest number of people in the Indies. The nationalists had the vision to see, however, the danger of jealousy on the part of all the non-Java people, the minorities from the other islands, and even the Sundanese and Madurese speakers on Java itself. If Javanese had been chosen there might well have been the kind of opposition seen in India, where large-scale "language riots" prevented Hindi from becoming the national language. This is not just a sentimental question. It is of practical importance in getting government jobs, for instance, because of the language used in civil service examinations.

But another objection to Javanese was that it was associated in the public mind with the upper classes. The aristocracy tended in former times to be the only people who were literate in Javanese, and so the language in written form seemed to be for aristocrats. And Javanese is a complex business anyway. There are three different forms of the language, for use when talking to superiors, to inferiors, and to people of your own class. That did not sound like the right way for people to talk in a democracy.

So the new national language based on Malay became more than just a means of communication. It is a symbol of nationhood, and one of the ways in which Indonesia binds together the different parts of its great country. Regional pride is still strong in Indonesia and a matter of much good-natured joking among friends, but the joking is in the national language.

Indonesia hopes to achieve the same sort of loyalty that is suggested in the national motto of their country and ours, implying mutual respect, understanding, and tolerance. It even involves pride in the different culture of fellow citizens in other parts of the country. A Muslim from Sumatra, for instance, takes pride in the Hindu dancing of Bali or the grace of the boats from Madura. A Javanese is delighted by the perfect design of folk art from Sulawesi or the charm of Minangkabau houses. People from all the islands thrill at the noble Hindu and Buddhist monuments in Java. Muslims in all the islands respect able public servants even though they are Christians from Sumatra. The whole nation honors its heroes from whatever section or religion or way of life.

In a number of ways the new country did poorly in the early years after independence, and in several areas the record was unsatisfactory for a long time. Production declined in various fields, and the economy fell into a sad state. The experience with political democracy failed to satisfy Indonesians, let alone critical foreigners. But in the field of education, progress was outstanding from the start.

The number of people able to read increased from 7 percent to more than 65 percent (for ages 10 to 49) in the first quarter century of the Republic's history. The number of elementary and secondary schools increased greatly, and at the same time universities, teachers' colleges, and technical schools grew up. And in some ways the most exciting development of all, adult "mass education" was undertaken throughout the country, much of it using the methods of "nonformal education."

One of the most important indexes of education in any country is the percentage of school-age children actually in school. Indonesia can now boast that more than 80 percent of its children of elementary-school age (7 to 12) are in school.

Nursery schools and kindergartens, once barely visible on the Indonesian scene, are now found in all provinces and are numbered

in the thousands. Most are sponsored by private societies and religious groups, and the largest number by associations of the wives of
government officials. They seem in general much like American
schools for children of the same age. They have programs of games,
singing, arts, and crafts. Most of the equipment seems to be very well
designed and constructed.

As in all Muslim countries, religious schools play a vital part in
the total educational system. The *madrassahs*, which might be called
Islamic parochial schools, are not, in Indonesia, substitutes for the
government schools but rather supplements to them. And for adults
there are many *pesantrens* or study centers attached to mosques or
otherwise maintained not only for pious Muslims who can go there
for learning and contemplation but also for use as community development centers.

In the regular government school system, which includes four-
fifths of the children of school age for the beginning grades, six years
of elementary school (ages 7 to 12) are followed by three years of
junior secondary (ages 13 to 15), and then three years of senior
secondary (ages 16 to 18). Although the number of young people
continuing to the end of the school years is rising, it is still quite
low—only 6 percent of those of senior high school age are actually
in school. Besides the pleasing figure for the children of elementary-
school age, another gratifying statistic is the rising number of girls
in high school. For a country where at one time virtually no girls
received education, it is quite creditable that two-fifths of all the
students in high school are girls. And incidentally, 30 percent of all
university students are women.

Many of the high schools are vocational schools, permitting the
start of professional training right after elementary school. Thus,
besides the regular schools, there are many that give special training
in commercial work, domestic science, mechanics, agriculture, social
work, and so forth.

In the elementary schools especially, but in the high schools

Students confronting a general in a protest incident

also, civics is a major subject. The subject gained special importance because of the effort at spreading grass-roots understanding of government plans.

As might be guessed, language has a large place in school studies. In some regions the teaching can be in the local language for the first two years, but the national Indonesian language is studied at the same time. After that, only the national language can be used for teaching. English and sometimes other foreign languages are subjects of study in high school.

There are fewer student activities than in our schools, but the Indonesians make up for this by the large number of youth groups sponsored by the government or by private associations under some kind of government direction or sponsorship. The Boy Scouts are especially active. In some cities there are organizations like our playground societies for singing, dance, music, and sports. Politics is a form of "student activity" that has been frequently evident on university campuses in recent years. Before, during, and after the coup of 1965, demonstrations by university students were major factors in defeating the Communists and deposing Sukarno, and since then student activists have demonstrated periodically to call attention to what they felt were abuses of power or misplaced government priorities.

Indonesians are not content with their schools yet. They are calling all the time for more school buildings, teachers, and books, and for making the quality of education better. Instead of being self-satisfied about the progress made in the first years of the Republic, they think the present school system is only a halfway point toward what they hope for later on. The foreigner, however, sees that to have built a national educational system at all is an accomplishment. It has drawn on efforts through the years by many different groups in Indonesia. And it gained from the work of foreign-trained Indonesians as well as foreign specialists sent on Indonesian request by other countries and foundations and by international organizations.

Going along with the great educational trend have been developments in the fields of newspapers, magazines, and book publishing. That work was once entirely Dutch directed, and not many Indonesians had previous experience in those fields. They took to the work very naturally, however, and until the economic problems at the end of the Sukarno period overcame them, impressive progress was made. The editors and publishers were courageous, and publishing survived in spite of economic hardship, paper shortage, inadequate maintenance of machinery, and government censorship.

Of the foreign books imported in the earlier years after independence, the largest number were from America, thanks to an arrangement by our government that permitted the Indonesians to buy American books with their own money, without having to pay in dollars. English-language books are still very popular in Indonesia, and American textbooks are used in quite a number of university courses. Translations of American books into Indonesian have likewise been published.

Dramatic technological changes in communication in Indonesia have come about through TV and the satellite—the first for any ASEAN country—that ties all sections to the rest of the country and the rest of the world. Helpful though that is in many ways, some Indonesians fear that this development might have harmful effects also, through subjecting the one-time local autonomy to easier central control.

As we noted above, the patriots leading the intellectual side of the independence movement made a big issue about the Indonesian language. But because there had been so long a period without an Indonesian literature, it was difficult to build one all of a sudden. There was no foundation of previous literature in the language. Older works—even by many of the active patriots—were usually in Dutch, and the aristocratic Javanese tradition of writing only for and about the upper classes was not much help. Censorship as well as economic hardship brought new problems to writers. But in spite of everything an Indonesian literature has been developing, and it now has a base. The most important need for a national literature has been supplied by the educational system: an audience able to read what is written.

13

Toward the Future

Through all the troubles that the country has survived—war, revolution, famine, military occupation, corruption, bureaucratic mismanagement, and power threats from both within and without—the incredible Indonesian people have shown courage, resilience, and faith in the future. It was the people themselves who won the battles. The leaders could not have accomplished anything without the commitment and support of the population as a whole.

Two Indonesian principles of great importance have been critical in the effort. One of these is *gotong royong*, or "mutual assistance." This principle is vitally alive. Foreign visitors see it in a small way in the almost universal habit of stopping to help people with broken-down autos. More important is the custom of helping village neighbors in trouble of any sort. In the hard struggle to get enough to eat, it is said that "a whole village might starve, but never a single individual."

The other basic principle that has helped Indonesia pull through difficulties is *musyawarah*, the process of deliberation. To an impatient foreigner musyawarah can seem like talking all the time without ever doing anything. To the Indonesian, however, it means patient consideration of all points of view and making sure of unanimous agreement before going ahead. Decisions are often postponed again and again, waiting for all to agree. Even in the matter of military control, which we will mention shortly, the process of musyawarah plays its role. That is, the military itself makes use of the methods of musyawarah in arriving at its decisions. Although a single peremptory order comes forth, that order itself may be the result of musyawarah among equals in the command group.

The passing of political power from President Sukarno to President Suharto after the attempted coup in 1965 was a golden example of Indonesian patience and deliberation. Many important figures, both civil and military, played leading roles. General Mohammed Jusuf, who later became Minister of Defense with wide admiration from many segments of Indonesian society, was one of the most important in handling the transfer. Among the civilians the most active in helping to establish the New Order were Adam Malik, who became Foreign Minister and then Vice-President; the Sultan of Yogyakarta, whom we met earlier; and Dr. Widjojo Nitisastro, the leading "technocrat" of both the former and the new administration.

Dr. Widjojo, a U.S.–trained economist and population specialist, was the leader of a group of a half-dozen or so brilliant social scientists who did graduate work at the University of California, mostly under Ford Foundation sponsorship. The group was jokingly called "the Berkeley Mafia." For a time after their return to Indonesia, some of them were not able to make full use of their talents. Dr. Widjojo, however, became director of the national planning agency called BAPPENAS, and was able to bring the rest of the group also into important positions in the planning process. He was in effect the chairman of the Suharto board of economic advisers, and it is now recognized that they were the architects of the country's truly remarkable economic development in the late 1960s and the 1970s.

There were other courageous and far-seeing builders, some in regional positions and one outstanding one in the national capital. This was Ali Sadikin, governor of Jakarta. He was a Mayor La-

Dr. Widjojo Nitisastro, Director of National Planning

General Mohammed Jusuf, one of Indonesia's most admired military figures

Guardia-type activist, determined to let no obstacle stand in the way of progress. When Ali Sadikin was appointed governor many people felt the city's problems were almost unsolvable, and that Jakarta was fated to be "the Calcutta of Southeast Asia." But when he left the office it was clear that Jakarta, while still having many problems, could be a livable modern city. This remarkable achievement won for Ali Sadikin the international recognition of a Magsaysay Award.

Economic growth under President Suharto has been sensational, and has been especially impressive because of the sad state of the economy when he took power. One of the greatest achievements, and one that brought benefits to the largest number of people, was the stabilization of the price of rice. But there were many other social and economic victories in addition. Both production and export of many commodities have increased, and foreign investment has been attracted. Although there has been some criticism, most of these activities have been along lines creating new economic wealth. The bonanza from increased oil prices has been wisely used for schools, clinics, roads, and markets.

In the social field, an outstanding achievement has been to get the family-planning movement really moving. It had started under private auspices several decades ago, and there was token adoption of the program by the Sukarno government. But it has been only under the New Order that the government program has taken hold throughout the country.

The biggest failure of the New Order has been its inability to curb the corruption that is admitted to flourish in almost all areas of public life. Corruption has been a special target of student activists and other young protesters. Their predecessor student groups had a major hand in bringing down Sukarno. When they turned their attention to human rights and the problem of corruption, it appeared for a time that they might accomplish genuine reform in those difficult areas, but the troublesome issues remain.

As the economic success of the New Order became clear, less use was made of internationally recognized holdover figures such as Sumitro, the economist, and Soedjatmoko, the former publisher and ambassador (and, incidentally, a member of the Ford Foundation board of trustees). They had been brought into the government soon after the change, and their recognition by the world's intellectual leadership made them especially useful to the Suharto government at that time.

Actually, under Adam Malik's direction, first as foreign minister and then as vice president, Indonesia has fared very well in international affairs in recent years, both on its own and as a member of ASEAN. Adam Malik was one of the chief organizers of ASEAN in 1967. At the beginning it seemed that ASEAN might be just one more regional group put together for appearance's sake. But it has taken on more and more reality and become one of the soundest regional groups anywhere. Genuine cooperation takes place among the five members—Indonesia, Thailand, Philippines, Malaysia, and Singapore—and ASEAN has come to have real influence in world affairs.

Military officers take part in nearly all phases of civic life, behind the scenes if not up front. Other groups play roles also—parties, trade unions, business, youth—but on a great many of the issues the military have the deciding voice. The political history of the New Order has been called a series of collapsing alliances. Students, intellectuals, and the Muslim groups that had helped Suharto to power gradually faded from the political arena. They formed the political party Golkar to help Suharto win his first election as president. But later the government reduced the existing eleven parties to just three: Golkar; PPP, a merger of the Muslim parties; and PDI, a merger of the Nationalist and Christian parties. And the armed forces were restructured in a way that made them less subject to influence by political parties and less likely to turn back toward the "regionalism" of the 1950s. At the same time a movement started toward shifting into less critical positions the military figures who had advocated radical changes from political practice. They were retired, moved to less sensitive offices, or otherwise neutralized.

The biggest fact of life in Indonesia, however, is not military power but the extent and pervasiveness of bureaucracy. Some countries are described as capitalist states or socialist states or democratic states or military dictatorships, but the one most accurate term for modern Indonesia is "a bureaucratic state." And as the bureaucracy has developed and spread its power, the dominance of the central government has increased. Better communication, though useful in many ways, has cut down regional independence. At least in matters of policy, provinces and other regional units have less freedom to go their own ways than they used to have.

At the bottom level, however—"down where people really live"—it appears that traditional processes of village democracy are still very much alive. Musyawarah continues to operate, and optimists think it will continue to thrive, no matter what happens at the higher political levels.

Indonesia, like so many other countries, faces the problem of the split between those with wealth and those without, and this has tended to encourage radical appeals to poor people to overturn the political system. Many of the protest incidents—such as the famous riots at the time of a visit by a Japanese prime minister in 1974— may seem to relate to other issues, but actually have their basis in urban poverty.

Politically, Indonesia's experiment with imported forms of democracy in the 1950s and 1960s has probably confirmed their natural inclination to structure civil life on their own unique Pancasila democracy. But however Indonesia finally settles its political affairs, it seems likely that there will be a large element of state control in many fields of activity, and that social services will be maintained by the government on a wide scale.

Indonesian nationalists felt in the past that they could not accept either straight capitalism, which they thought limited eco-

President Suharto

nomic freedom, or Marxist socialism that denied freedom to the individual. They wanted, in time-honored Indonesian style, to see if they could work out a new system all their own, drawing something from both.

The country has great natural strengths not only of a material sort, including natural resources, but of heart and mind and spirit also. The condition of "unity in diversity" of this country of islands is in itself an asset of great value. The nation's physical, cultural, and economic variety seems to many people to be a bastion against totalitarianism. The tradition of musyawarah and the five principles of the Pancasila (of which belief in God is the first) will continue to serve Indonesia well in the future as they did during the difficult times of the past. We should not expect these admirable and attractive people to construct a system like ours. We built ours out of our history and special conditions.

May they do the same, finding a plan which works well in their terms and gives human dignity to its citizens and full life for the individual in his body, mind, and spirit.

Suggestions for Further Reading

Vicki Baum. *A Tale of Bali.* The famous novelist based this book on a draft of a Dutch novel about the suicidal last stand of some Balinese nobles against Dutch conquest in the 1904–6 period. Her view of Dutch rule in Indonesia was more favorable than most observers would accept today, but the picture of daily rural life in Bali is meticulously accurate and memorable. Published by Oxford/Kuala Lumpur, but can be ordered through Oxford/New York.

Agnes De Keijzer Brackman. *Cook Indonesian.* A practical cookbook published in Singapore but available in U.S. from Hippocrene Books, New York.

James R. Brandon. *Theatre in Southeast Asia.* Harvard University Press. Paperback. Illustrated. The best overall treatment, scholarly but easily read by laymen.

Bill Dalton. *Indonesian Handbook.* A 486-page paperback guidebook with the shortcomings of such works but crammed with useful facts. Published in Singapore but available in the United States from Charles Tuttle, Rutland, Vermont.

Clifford Geertz. *The Religion of Java.* Free Press. Heavy going for the lay reader but the most important Western study of the subject.

D. G. E. Hall. *A History of South-East Asia.* St. Martin's Press. A 1,070-page paperback, the most comprehensive one-volume treatment of the whole region.

John Hughes. *Indonesian Upheaval.* An account of the 1965 change of government, by the former editor of the *Christian Science Monitor*, who had won a Pulitzer Prize for the reportage on which this book is based.

Raden Adjeng Kartini. *Letters of a Javanese Princess.* Norton. Paperback. A literary masterpiece that is delightful for modern readers. See our comment about this on pp. 89–90 of this book.

Colin McPhee. *A House in Bali.* AMS Press. A personal picture of life in Bali in the 1930s.

Wilfred T. Neill. *Twentieth Century Indonesia.* Columbia University Press. Paperback. The history in the last third of the book is better handled elsewhere, but this work gives an invaluable description of the natural setting, especially fauna, flora, and resources.

James L. Peacock. *Indonesia: An Anthropological Perspective.* Goodyear. An excellent general view of Indonesian anthropology.

M. C. Ricklefs. *A History of Modern Indonesia.* Indiana University Press. Of the many general histories, this, by an Australian scholar, is perhaps the most useful for general readers.

Sutan Sjahrir. *Out of Exile.* Greenwood Press. See our comment about this famous work on p. 72 of this book.

Bernard H. M. Vlekke. *Nusantara: A History of Indonesia.* This is one of the most fair-minded, readable, and useful of the many histories of the Indies by Dutch scholars. Out of print but well worth looking up in the libraries that have it in either the original edition or a special Arno reprint.

Frits A. Wagner. *Indonesia: The Art of an Island Group.* A beautifully illustrated presentation of both visual and performing arts. Out of print but the time spent looking it up in libraries (especially art libraries or Southeast Asia collections) that still have it will be richly rewarded.

Acknowledgments

For assistance in preparing this revised edition, the author is indebted to more friends, in Indonesia and elsewhere, than can be named here, but a few must be specially mentioned.

For overall criticism and suggestions, the author is deeply obligated to two people. One is his daughter, Karen Houston Smith of Unicef, who is Indonesia's wisest friend and most clear-eyed interpreter among all Americans. The other is Ismid Hadad, former editor of *Prisma* of Jakarta, a staff member of LP3ES, the Institute for Economic and Social Research, Education, and Information.

For valuable assistance on musical subjects, he thanks Professor Hewitt Pantaleoni of the State University of New York, Oneonta.

For friendly help through many years in securing Indonesian reference materials, he has continuing gratitude to Hassan and Julia Shadily of Jakarta.

It goes without saying that errors or misinterpretations remaining in the book are the fault of the author alone.

Photo Credits

Boston Museum of Fine Arts, the picture on p. 23.

Ford Foundation, the picture on p. 86.

Directorate-General of Tourism, Ministry of Transport, Communication, and Tourism, Government of Indonesia, the pictures on pp. 5, 7, 17, 75, 107, 115, 118.

Foto Kempen, the pictures on pp. 4, 10, 13, 16, 26, 34, 50, 51, 53, 64, 72, 73, 83, 99, 102, 111, 112, 116, 120, 122.

Foto Tempo, the pictures on pp. 6, 71, 84, 90, 92, 104, 131, 136, 139.

Index

About the Author

Datus C. Smith, Jr., has been a friend and observer of Indonesia for more than thirty years. He is director of book publishing of the Asia Society and was formerly director of Princeton University Press and president of Franklin Book Programs, one of whose operating offices was in Jakarta. He has served as president of the U.S. Committee for Unicef and of the United States Board on Books for Young People.